WORD PROCESSING FOR COLLEGE WRITERS

AF713746

WORD PROCESSING FOR COLLEGE WRITERS

Hadley M. Smith
Ithaca College

Mary Lynch Kennedy
SUNY College at Cortland

PRENTICE HALL, Englewood Cliffs, New Jersey 07632

Library of Congress Cataloging-in-Publication Data

Smith, Hadley M., (date)
Word processing for college writers / Hadley M. Smith, Mary Lynch Kennedy.
p. cm.
Includes index.
ISBN 0-13-964503-9
1. English language—Rhetoric—Data processing. 2. Word processing in education. I. Kennedy, Mary Lynch. II. Title.
PE1408.S596 1989
808'.042'0285416—dc19 88-29010
CIP

Apple is a registered trademark of Apple Computer, Inc.

CP/M is a registered trademark of Digital Research.

IBM is a registered trademark of International Business Machines Corporation.

Macintosh is a trademark of Apple Computer, Inc.

MS-DOS is a registered trademark of the Microsoft Corporation.

Cover design: *Diane Saxe*
Manufacturing buyer: *Laura Crossland*

© 1989 by Prentice-Hall, Inc.
A Division of Simon & Schuster
Englewood Cliffs, New Jersey 07632

All rights reserved. No part of this book may be reproduced, in any form or by any means, without permission in writing from the publisher.

Printed in the United States of America

10 9 8 7 6 5 4 3 2 1

ISBN 0-13-964503-9

Prentice-Hall International (UK) Limited, *London*
Prentice-Hall of Australia Pty. Limited, *Sydney*
Prentice-Hall Canada Inc., *Toronto*
Prentice-Hall Hispanoamericana, S.A., *Mexico*
Prentice-Hall of India Private Limited, *New Delhi*
Prentice-Hall of Japan, Inc., *Tokyo*
Simon & Schuster Asia Pte. Ltd., *Singapore*
Editora Prentice-Hall do Brasil, Ltda., *Rio de Janeiro*

To Nancy

—H.M.S.

To Bill

—M.L.K.

CONTENTS

PREFACE: TO THE INSTRUCTOR

Today, many college students have access to word processors, but there are few textbooks that explain how they can take full advantage of these devices as they do their academic work. Research suggests that having students write on word processors does not, in and of itself, make them better writers. They need explicit instruction on how word processors can be used as writing tools. *Word Processing for College Writers* provides this instruction. It shows students how word processing can assist them at each of the major stages in the writing process: planning, drafting, revising, and editing. Although this book stresses a computer-based approach to the writing process, it does not oversimplify this process, nor does it present word processing as a panacea for all writing difficulties. Rather, it keeps word processing in perspective as a supplement to the writer's traditional tools.

This textbook goes beyond using word processors as convenient editing tools and emphasizes how the technology can help students explore structural and stylistic alternatives. Too often, students and instructors become so entranced with the editing capabilities of word processors that they fail to recognize their machines' potential for helping to explore topics and to undertake global revision. Although computers cannot actually suggest novel ideas or alternative organizational strategies, they do make practical the experimentation that leads to innovation. A major goal of this text is to encourage experimentation at all stages of the writing process.

Word Processing for College Writers is a very flexible text. It can be used by first-year students and upperclass students alike since it avoids computer jargon by employing straightforward prose that all college students can understand. The book can serve as a major text for a writing course that focuses on word processing, or it can serve as an adjunct text in a freshman composition or advanced writing course. In addition, it can be used as a resource handbook for *any* college course in which students use word processors to write papers. After reading Chapter 1, students can use the rest of the chapters in the text individually or in a sequence different from that suggested in the table of contents. The book is not hardware or software specific. It can be used in conjunction with any computer and any word processing program.

In preparing *Word Processing for College Writers* we relied on the work of many researchers in composition and word processing. In particular, we would like to note the work of Hugh Burns, Colette Daiute, Jeanette Harris, Stephen Marcus, Dawn Wilson Rodrigues, Raymond J. Rodrigues, Helen Schwartz, Cynthia L. Selfe, and William Wresch. At Ithaca College our colleagues Barbara Adams and Lary Jones contributed their computer expertise to the project. A special thanks is due William J. Kennedy for his insightful comments and generous help in revising the manuscript. At Prentice Hall we were privileged to work with Editor-in-Chief Phil Miller and his assistant Jane Bauman, English Editor Lynne Greenberg, and our regional representative Jennifer Plane. We are indebted to our reviewers, who contributed their ideas and insightful analysis: Craig Etchinson, Glenville State College; Frank Madden, Westchester Community College; Roger Schlobin, Purdue University; Tom Sullivan, Moraine Valley Community College; and William Wresch, University of Wisconsin at Stevens Point. Finally, we want to recognize William, Liam, and Maura Kennedy, Nancy Siegele, and Annie and Colin Smith for their patience, support, and understanding.

WORD PROCESSING FOR COLLEGE WRITERS

ONE
WORD PROCESSING AND WRITING: AN INTRODUCTION

WHAT THIS TEXTBOOK WILL DO

The computer revolution has happened, and more and more writers are using word processors instead of typewriters, pencils, and pens. Computers have replaced typewriters in homes, businesses, and schools, and a generation of children is rapidly learning "electronic" writing. If you have not yet discovered the advantages of word processors, this book will inform you. It explains how word processors can help you become a more efficient and successful writer.

In this book, we use the term *word processing* to refer to computer-assisted writing in general. Used in this sense, word processing describes activities that can be carried out on mainframe computers, microcomputers, and modern electronic typewriters, as well as on machines that are designed and marketed specifically as word processors. In the foreseeable future writers at colleges and in the workplace will have access to a wide variety of machinery and programs as they compose and revise. No matter what software package or computer system they use, however, they will benefit from word processing in similar ways. It is these common features of word processors that we discuss in this text.

Even if you have no prior experience with computers, you should not be intimidated by word processing technology. We have known many students and professors who suffered from computer phobia and had long refused to use word processors. Even so, when they made the effort, they learned how to use word processors after only a few hours of instruction and practice. Granted, they did not learn every function their word processors offered. This is not necessary for beginners. Later in this chapter we list the particular functions that novices must know. Plunge in and familiarize yourself with these basic operations. Then you will be able to use this textbook with ease.

You will find this text more accessible than word processor manuals because we rely as much as possible on the standard vocabulary typically used to discuss writing, rather than on computer jargon. Nonetheless, you will need to learn how your particular word processor operates, either from the manufacturer's manual or from an instructor or student who knows the program. Indeed, there are so many different word processing programs on the market that no one text could possibly teach writers how to use all of them. Instead of repeating the mechanics that your manual describes, we will try to show how using those mechanics can improve your writing. We will focus on the features that most word processors and many electronic typewriters offer. Certainly, many highly sophisticated word processors have features designed specifically for college writing. For instance, some word processors provide stylistic advice, and others allow the writer to handle citations and reference notes easily. These sophisticated programs vary greatly, however, and it is doubtful that a single program will emerge as a nationwide standard. Many individuals and institutions have already invested substantial sums of money in programs that they intend to use for many years. Because of these factors, we explain how to use the basic features common to most word processors instead of trying to describe all the capabilities of individual programs.

Finally, we should point out that this textbook is by no means a complete guide to writing. It is designed to be used in conjunction with other instructional materials and reference books. It certainly cannot replace the traditional resources of a college writer: a good dictionary and a comprehensive handbook of rhetoric and style. We will show you how word processing can help you use these resources to better advantage, but you will still need to refer to them as you write. If you are using this book in a writing course, it will most likely be a supplement to a standard writing textbook that covers the steps in the writing process—prewriting, drafting, revising, and editing—in more detail than we do here. Throughout the book we will refer often to other instructional materials that we assume you are using simultaneously.

HOW WORD PROCESSORS HELP COLLEGE WRITERS

At the outset we must stress that with or without computers, writing is hard work. Word processing technology may make certain operations easier, but it does not simplify the basic writing process. Whether they use computers or pencils, it is writers who make all the important decisions and direct all the writing activities. If you look to this book primarily for shortcuts, for ways to make writing effortless, you will probably be disappointed. On the other hand, if you are interested in using current technology to improve your writing, this book is for you.

Many people think of word processors as machines that correct errors. Certainly, that is an important function of the technology: It allows you to correct errors and add or delete reconsidered material without typing a whole new copy. Word processing can help you to do more than edit and revise, however. It can aid in the entire process of writing papers for college courses, from the first day you receive the assignment to the day you hand in the final printed draft. It can allow you to think about the entire writing process of planning, drafting, revising, and editing, rather than focusing exclusively on the finished paper. If you have felt bogged down by planning and revision and found it difficult to complete a single draft of your paper, let alone an initial outline and multiple revisions, the word processor can help you. Computers make it easier to complete the steps in the writing process, and they can reduce the frustration of planning, drafting, revising, and editing. We have organized this book to show you how word processing can enhance the full range of writing activities.

First, we will discuss briefly the four basic activities that writing involves: planning, drafting, revising, and editing. Then in successive chapters we will demonstrate how word processing can assist you with these activities as you work on writing assignments in your college courses.

The Process of Writing

Before we review the writing process, we want to remind you that even though we discuss planning, drafting, revising, and editing in successive stages, these processes do not necessarily occur in this order. Writers seldom proceed in a lockstep fashion from planning to editing. The various stages of writing intermix. For example, many writers make revisions while they are composing, as well as after they have completed a full draft. In this book we will show you how word processing makes it easy to shift back and forth among planning, drafting, revising, and editing activities as you write.

Planning

Skilled writers often spend much more time planning than drafting. On the other hand, some less able writers do very little planning. What does the planning of expert writers entail? Planning may include brainstorming, listing, and freewriting, techniques writers use to stimulate invention by calling up their own knowledge of a topic. College writers usually need to demonstrate academic learning in addition to general knowledge, experience, or personal judgment. Consequently, their planning includes reading activities, such as researching, note taking, annotating sources, self-questioning, and mapping. In all cases planning also involves focusing, arranging, and structuring the material the writer has invented, discovered, or read. In Chapters 2 and 3 we will explain planning activities in detail.

Drafting

Drafting forces you to examine your own thoughts and the ideas you have obtained from readings and other sources, and it requires you to communicate them to a reader in sentences and paragraphs that follow an organizational plan. Most likely, your planning-stage notes will be sketchy. In the first draft of your paper you will flesh out the ideas in these notes and arrange the material logically so that the reader of your paper can follow your train of thought. In Chapter 4 we will discuss drafting.

Revising

Writers revise as they compose, as well as after they have completed a draft. As you write, you will find yourself stopping frequently to reread sentences or paragraphs and cross out or add material. After you complete a draft, you may also make more substantial changes, such as recasting the overall organization of the paper, rearranging the order of sentences and paragraphs, deleting and adding sentences and paragraphs, and even modifying the thesis statement. You may likewise decide to alter the content of your paper or the way you have used or documented sources. Depending on the assignment and your own work habits, you may produce several preliminary drafts before you are ready to write the final version. Save all the drafts because your professor may require you to hand them in along with the finished product.

For many students, revising does not come easy. They cannot locate their problem areas and errors because they have not learned how to stand back and analyze their work objectively. In Chapters 5, 6, and 7 we will show you how to become your own reader, how to read your drafts critically, react to them, and make meaningful changes.

Editing

Editing involves locating and correcting errors in grammar, spelling, and mechanics. As with revising, writers edit both during and after the process of drafting. Perhaps the most obvious advantage of word processors is that they make editing much easier. In Chapter 8 we will describe this advantage in detail.

COMPUTERS AND THE WRITING PROCESS

For centuries, writers have planned, drafted, revised, and edited, in earlier times using pens and pencils and more recently using typewriters as their writing tools. Indeed, you still need these tools to write well today. Word processors do not make them obsolete, but computers can assist writers in ways that the traditional tools cannot. The rest of this book will show how word processing technology can help you with your college writing.

In this book we focus on specific ways that word processing can help you at each stage of the writing process. Keep in mind that word processing will help you most if it allows you to establish more control over the *entire* process. Too often, students do not recognize their responsibilities as writers. They may scribble a first draft, pass it before the eyes of an instructor or writing center tutor, and then give it to a typist and hope for the best. Word processing allows students to exercise command over all aspects of the writing process, from generating ideas to producing the final draft. As students establish more control over this process, they will become better writers.

Another general advantage of word processing is that it allows writers to experiment with alternative approaches to writing tasks. Often, college writers greatly limit their exploration of ideas because of the sheer drudgery of note taking, writing, revising, and editing. Word processing can streamline these activities so that they are easier and less time-consuming, leaving the writer with more time and energy for experimentation. For example, the computer enables you to produce three or four printed versions of the same paper, each structured according to a different organizational pattern. Exploring alternatives so freely is not practical if you are using a pencil or a typewriter. One of our main goals is to encourage the free play with ideas, organization, and language that word processors make possible.

As you work through the chapters, keep in mind that our goal is to help you become a better writer, not a technophile. If you give word processing a try and still find that pencils and typewriters work better for you, then by all means use the writing tools with which you are more comfortable. Also remember that word processing facilitates writing but does not teach you how to write and certainly does not write for you. If you use the word processor intelligently, it can help you to develop your writing in the directions you want it to go.

WHAT YOU NEED TO KNOW ABOUT YOUR WORD PROCESSOR IN ORDER TO USE THIS BOOK

Most modern word processors are relatively easy to use. With a few hours of study and practice, even someone who has never touched a computer keyboard can draft, revise, edit, and print out papers. To learn how your particular word processor works, read its accompanying manual, or better yet, get help from a friend, instructor, or tutor in your campus writing center, learning laboratory, or computing service. This book will not explain how to operate the many brands of word processors. Its aim is to show you how you can use the basic features of a word processor to facilitate your writing.

You do not have to learn the specialized operations of sophisticated word processing programs. To use the bulk of this textbook, all you need to

BASIC WORD PROCESSOR FUNCTIONS

- Starting up your word processing program and exiting from the program
- Establishing a textfile to store your paper
- Typing in your paper
- Saving your textfile
- Retrieving your paper from storage
- Adding, deleting, substituting, rearranging, and duplicating
- Handling several textfiles simultaneously (if available)
- Using search-and-replace commands (if available)
- Scanning your paper with a spelling checker (if available)
- Printing your paper
- Backing up your work

know are the features of your word processor that we described below. Make sure that you understand all these operations *before* you proceed. The most basic word processors may not deliver the operations we have labeled "if available"; however, you should learn to use these features if you have them.

Starting Up Your Word Processing Program and Exiting from the Program

Before you attempt to use a word processor, make sure that you understand fully the startup and exiting procedures for your specific program.

Many college students do word processing on microcomputer systems that store information on *diskettes*. Startup procedures for these systems involve inserting one or more diskettes into the computer's *disk drives*. Microcomputers typically use 5¼ inch *floppy diskettes* or 3½ inch *hardshell diskettes*. Check your microcomputer manual to see what kind of diskette your machine requires. In most cases you will need to purchase a personal diskette before you do any word processing so that you will have a place to store your work. While you are actually typing on a word processor, the

FIGURE 1. A floppy diskette being inserted into a disk drive.

machine saves your work in its internal memory, but this memory is wiped out when you either exit from the word processing program or turn off the power. The microcomputer system will not save your work automatically, but if you copy your work on your personal diskette before you end a word processing session, you will be able to return to your work at a later session.

When you start with a new personal diskette, you will need to *initialize* or *format* it before you attempt to use it with your word processor. Initializing sets up the storage space on the diskette according to a pattern appropriate for your specific computer and software. Your word processor manual will explain how to initialize diskettes. *You cannot store papers on a diskette until it has been initialized for your particular word processor.* You need to initialize a diskette only once, however. *Note that formatting a diskette automatically erases any information that was put on the diskette previously.* Thus, if you store a paper on a diskette and then initialize the diskette again, the paper will be lost. Be careful not to initialize a diskette that already contains useful information.

Some word processing programs have an option that allows you to initialize diskettes, and some do not. If your word processor does not format diskettes, you may need to consult the manual that comes with your operating system (CP/M, MS-DOS, and so on).

Startup procedures typically begin with inserting into the disk drives both a personal diskette and a diskette that contains the word processing program. The word processing program will start when you turn on the power to the microcomputer. Although hardware varies, a microcomputer system often has two disk drives, one for the program diskette (usually "Drive A" or "Drive 1") and one for a personal diskette (usually "Drive B" or "Drive 2"). Make sure you understand which diskette needs to be in each disk drive before you start your computer. Unless there is a reason to change diskettes, do not remove them until the end of the word processing session since the computer may periodically read information from the program diskette, and you may need to read from and write to your personal diskette. One common cause of lost work is failing to insert the necessary diskettes; another is removing of the diskettes prematurely.

If you are working on a mainframe computer or a microcomputer with a *hard disk,* you may not need diskettes for startup. These computers have large internal storage systems that have room for dozens of programs, and thus word processing software is often lodged within the computer's memory. You can easily retrieve the word processing program directly from memory. Either refer to your computer manual or check with the staff of your computer workroom to get the exact startup procedure for the machine you are using. *Also find out exactly where and how to save your work.* If you are using a mainframe computer, most likely you can save your work in the computer's memory system. On a hard disk microcomputer you can save work in the machine's internal memory, but you may want to keep your work on a personal diskette, particularly if you are sharing a machine with many different users. In any case, make sure you know how you will save your work before you begin a word processing session.

Most word processors have built-in exiting procedures that safeguard against losing work. Typically, the user is reminded to save any new work that was produced during the word processing session. Learn the exiting procedure for your word processor and take advantage of it. Never remove your diskettes until you have saved all your work and exited.

Establishing a Textfile to Store Your Paper

An important advantage of using a word processor is that the computer can store the typed version of a paper for revision at a later time. Thus, you need not draft, revise, edit, and print out a finished paper in one typing session. Instead, you can store your work and return to it another day. The computer stores your writing in a "textfile." All word processors allow the user to create and give names to textfiles. When you save a textfile on a diskette or in another memory system, the textfile is indexed according to the name you gave it when you first created it on the word processor. We will discuss storage procedures in more detail in a later section.

Make sure that you understand how your word processor creates textfiles. Most word processors force you to create and name a textfile before you can type in anything at all. Make sure that you choose a textfile name that will help you remember the contents of the file. You may need to abbreviate since many computer systems limit the lengths of the textfile names. For example, a paper on Shakespeare's sonnets might be named "*SHAKES*" or "*SONNET*."

Typing In Your Paper

Don't shy away from word processors just because you have never typed before. We have found that with a little practice, students with no typing background are soon able to master the skills to type three- to five-page papers. Since novice typists can correct errors so much more easily with word processors than with conventional typewriters, they need not worry about accuracy. Even reluctant typists pick up speed and confidence quickly once they begin to work with the word processor. For those who prefer formal typing instruction, programs that teach touch typing are available for virtually all computer systems.

Once you have created a textfile and you begin to type your paper on the word processor, the machine operates as a typewriter does, but with two significant differences. Most word processors have a feature called "automatic word wrap." As you type, the program will automatically insert a carriage return when you reach the end of each line. Thus, you do not have to worry about shifting to a new line when you type. The program will determine the length of each line based on preset margin widths. If you do nothing to change the margin width, most word processors will automatically leave one-inch margins on all sides. A second important difference between typewriters and word processors is that word processors allow you to revise more extensively as you produce the first draft. They offer much greater flexibility than typewriters. We will discuss this advantage later in the book.

As you experiment with typing on your word processor, learn how to control the appearance of your work on the printed page. Usually, word processors have built-in specifications for margin width, typeface, letter spacing, and other layout features, but often you can change these specifications easily. You will probably find that most of these built-in specifications are close to what you want for academic work, for example the one-inch margins we mentioned earlier. Nevertheless, you will probably need to make some changes. Many word processors are set up to print single-spaced lines, whereas college professors usually require double-spaced papers. Make sure you know how to control line spacing. You should also determine how your word processor numbers pages. Some word processing programs make page numbering so awkward that it may be easier to turn off the automatic page numbering and use a typewriter to number the pages in the final draft. Finally, learn how to insert an end-of-page command in your paper. The end-of-page command forces the word processor to begin a new page even though the current page is not full. You will need this command to end title pages and to separate the text of a source paper from the list of references.

In general, keep the layout of your paper simple. Make it look as much as possible like a paper done on a typewriter. If your word processor is set up to space the words on each line so that the right margin is even (right justification), turn off this feature and leave a ragged right margin. Do not overwork features, such as boldface print or italics, that are not available on conventional typewriters. Learn how to make your word processor underline individual words in printed drafts.

Saving Your Textfile

Many beginners fear that the word processor will erase all their work after they have spent a lot of time typing it. You can avoid disastrous losses by carefully saving your textfile about every fifteen minutes as you type, in addition to saving your completed draft at the end of the word processing session. "Saving" refers to the process of storing a copy of your work in some permanent storage device, typically a diskette or a computer's internal memory system. Once you save a textfile, you can retrieve it at a later time and add to, revise, edit, or print it. Make sure you understand how to store the textfiles that you create on your word processor. Practice the procedure and become familiar with all aspects of it before you actually use the computer for your academic work.

As we mentioned above, you should save your work not only when you are done typing but also every fifteen minutes or so during long typing sessions. There is no limit to the number of times you can save a textfile, and in general, the more you save, the less chance you will have of losing your work. If you need to leave the keyboard temporarily, save the work before you leave, even though you intend to return soon and continue typing. This precaution is especially important in a computer workroom, where another user may mistakenly think you are finished. But even if you are working in the privacy of your own room, it is good practice to save your work before leaving your machine.

Diskettes are a reliable form of storage as long as you treat them carefully. Read the warning printed on the diskette packaging. Take care that you keep your diskette in its paper or cardboard cover whenever it is not in the computer. Carrying an unprotected diskette in a book bag or notebook will very likely damage it. Transport your diskette in a rigid plastic case. As we mentioned earlier, you cannot store your work on a new diskette until you have initialized or formatted it. Be sure to initialize an empty diskette, not one that already contains work you want to retain.

Retrieving Your Paper from Storage

You will often need to retrieve a textfile. The names of textfiles are listed in the directory of your diskette or computer memory system. Most word processors allow you to see the directory list as soon as you start up the program. You can then select the textfile you want to retrieve.

Adding, Deleting, Substituting, Rearranging, and Duplicating

It is easy to revise and edit your work on a word processor because you can move the *cursor* to any place in your paper in order to make a change. The cursor is the blinking bar that marks the location at which your next keystroke will take effect. Make sure you know how to control the cursor on your word processor. You should be able to move it both forward and backward through your paper. Most word processors have single keystroke commands for moving the cursor a letter, a word, a line, a sentence, or a page at a time. In many cases a single keystroke also sends the cursor to either the beginning or the end of the entire paper. Learn *all* possible ways to move the cursor. If you can manipulate the cursor efficiently, you will find it much easier to revise and edit your work.

Once you position the cursor, you can add material at that point in your draft. You can insert letters, words, sentences, or whole paragraphs.

When you insert new material, you never need to recopy parts of the earlier draft as you often do with handwritten or typed drafts. Just as you can insert new material, you can also delete material from the earlier draft without recopying the surrounding text. Many word processors let you use a single keystroke to delete a letter, a word, a line, a sentence, or a block of text within boundaries you specify. You can also combine adding and deleting operations to replace material in the earlier draft with new material. Another revision you may wish to make is changing the sequence of words, sentences, paragraphs, or larger sections of text. Most word processors make this revision with relative ease. You need only to indicate the boundaries of the material you want to move and then specify its new location. This operation is sometimes called "cut and paste" in word processor manuals.

Cut-and-paste procedures also make it possible for you to duplicate sentences or paragraphs. Duplication can be very helpful when you are revising and editing. For example, you can reproduce a problematic paragraph, change one copy, and then compare your new version to the original to see if you have actually made improvements. You can continue the process until you are satisfied with one version and ready to erase the rest. Make sure you understand how you can duplicate material on your word processor.

Handling Several Files Simultaneously

Many word processors will allow you to load two or more textfiles into the word processor so that you can work with several textfiles at the same time. If your program has this capability, learn how to use it. Different word processing programs implement this feature in a variety of ways. With some programs, the writer can divide the screen in half and display two different textfiles simultaneously in the separate halves of the screen. The writer can then shift the cursor back and forth between the two halves of the screen and move material from one textfile to the other. With other programs the writer can transfer several different textfiles into *windows* that can be "opened" and "closed" at various locations on the screen. The writer can display material from two or more textfiles at once and can control its arrangement on the screen. Still other programs let the writer store various textfiles in a series of *buffers* and then shift rapidly from buffer to buffer. No matter how the feature is implemented, the ability to work with several textfiles simultaneously is very helpful. At both the drafting and revising stages, it allows the writer to switch quickly back and forth between notes and various drafts of a paper. Make sure you know how to cut and paste material from one textfile to another and how to merge two textfiles.

Using Search-and-Replace Commands

Many but not all word processors have "search-and-replace" capabilities. These features are important editing tools because they enable you to search your entire paper for every instance of a particular word or a series of words or letters. For example, if you know that you have a tendency to confuse *their* and *there,* you can direct the computer to search your paper for all instances of these two words and then decide in each case whether or not you have used the correct form. You can also command the computer to replace the target letters or word(s) with new material. If, for instance, you habitually write "alot" you can command it to automatically replace it with "a lot." Word processores vary greatly in how they implement search-and-replace procedures, so refer to your manual for a more detailed explanation. If you have a choice of word processors, try to select one that has search-and-replace capabilities.

Scanning Your Paper with a Spelling Checker

A spelling checker if available is a useful editing tool. If you are a weak speller, the advantage is obvious, but even if spelling is one of your strengths, the spelling checker can catch typing errors that you might miss while proofreading. In addition, spelling checkers often have other helpful features, such as word counters.

Some spelling checkers are built into the word processing programs; others require separate pieces of software. They vary greatly in terms of features and ease of operation. If you have a choice of spelling checkers, pick the one that is fastest at the operations that interest you. Poor spelling checkers are so slow and inefficient that students find it easier to proofread without the computer's help. If you find your spelling checker is so slow or frustrating that you are not actually using it, try another program.

Printing Your Paper

Make sure that you know how to send a paper from the word processor to the printer so you can get a printed copy of your work. Remember to make your final draft look as much as possible like work done on a conventional typewriter. If possible, use a daisy-wheel printer for your final draft. If you are using a dot-matrix printer, insert a new ribbon and select the letter-quality option if you have it. Even if you are typing in a computer workroom, learn the basics of operating the printer. You should know how to adjust the paper so that the printer will begin at the top of the page rather than halfway down. Learn how to feed new paper into the printer in case the supply runs out in the middle of your project. Above all, anticipate printer problems: Printers break down much more frequently than computers do.

Save your work in permanent storage *before* you attempt to print it. With certain combinations of hardware and software, word processor files may be lost en route to the printer. This danger is greatest in computer workrooms, where several microcomputers are linked through a switchbox to a single printer. You can minimize the danger by making sure that the computer and the printer are properly connected and that the printer is switched on and loaded with paper before you try to print your file. Saving the textfile first gives you a backup copy in case the printing process does go awry.

Backing Up Your Work

Even the most careful writer may at some time lose either part or all of the information on a diskette. The diskette itself may be defective, or an accident, such as coffee spill, may destroy it. Periodically make backup copies of each diskette on which you store writing. In the computer industry the standard is to keep at least three separate backups for important work. Consult your operating system manual for information on how to make backup copies of your diskettes. If your microcomputer has a hard disk, you still need to copy all important files to diskettes so that you will have backups. Your owner's manual will explain how to back up a hard disk. If you are working on a mainframe computer system, check with the computer specialists at your college to see if they periodically back up the entire system. If they do not, you may need to have them copy your important files onto magnetic tape. In addition to copying entire diskettes, you can use your operating system to copy a single textfile from one diskette to another. Sometimes it is more convenient to back up a particular paper by copying only the textfile it is lodged in rather than the whole diskette.

In addition to backing up diskettes and textfiles periodically, it is a good idea to print out copies of your work after each session on the word processor. This provides another backup copy of your work. In addition, as you will see, there are some advantages to revising and editing your work on a printed copy as well as on the computer screen.

A CHECKLIST FOR WORD PROCESSING SESSIONS

If you use the following checklist, you can avoid common word processing difficulties. Note that some of the items on this checklist will not apply if your word processing system does not use diskettes.

WORD PROCESSING SESSION CHECKLIST

As you begin a word processing session:

- If you are starting with a new personal diskette make sure it has been initialized.
- Place all diskettes (personal and program) in the appropriate disk drives.
- Check to see that the capital letter lock is off.

During a word processing session:

- Save your work every fifteen minutes.
- Use textfile names that will help you remember the content of each file.
- Do not leave the keyboard, even temporarily, without saving your work.
- Save all your work before printing.
- Make sure the printer is turned on and that the computer and printer are connected before you give the print command.

As you end a word processing session:

- Follow the recommended procedures for exiting from your progam.
- Make backup copies of your diskettes periodically.
- Transport your diskettes in rigid plastic containers and protect them from dust, moisture, heat, and cold.

EXERCISE 1

The following revising and editing exercise will help familiarize you with the word processing operations we have described in this chapter. On your word processor *freewrite* nonstop for ten minutes on a topic of your choice. You might explain how you think word processing could help you to improve your writing, but any topic will do. Freewriting, a process we will describe in detail in Chapter 2, involves writing informally and expressing your ideas on a given topic without worrying about matters of correctness and style. Name the textfile for this exercise "Freewrite". After you have finished your freewriting, perform the following operations:

- Move the cursor to the begining of the "Freewrite" textfile. Insert a title page with your name, the course title, and the instructor's name. End the title page with a command that will direct the printer to begin a new page.
- Switch the order of the first and second paragraphs. If your first draft is only one paragraph, arbitrarily divide it into two paragraphs and then reverse their order.
- Combine the first and second paragraphs so that they now form a single paragraph.
- Delete the last two sentences of the passage.
- Use a comma and a conjunction (*and, but, for, or, nor, yet, so*) to combine the last two sentences in the final paragraph.
- Move the first sentence of the first paragraph to the end of the paragraph.
- Duplicate the last sentence in the passage.
- Add a new sentence immediately before the last sentence in the passage.
- Substitute a synonym for the first noun in the first sentence. Try another noun if the first one is problematic.
- Use your search-and-replace feature to substitute *are* for every occurence of *is* in your passage.
- Use a spelling checker to correct any errors in spelling.
- Store the "Freewrite" textfile on a diskette or other storage device.
- Exit from your word processor and turn off the computer.
- Restart the word processor and bring the passage back up on the screen.
- Print out a double-spaced version of the passage.
- Make a backup copy of the diskette that contains "Freewrite."

TWO
INVENTING AND COLLECTING IDEAS

WORD PROCESSORS AND INVENTION

You may think of invention as the act of exercising one's imagination to make a startling new discovery. Invention can also mean the process of finding what you want to say, of choosing ideas appropriate for your topic. We speak of "finding" and "choosing" rather than "creating" because often the ideas you need are already stored in your head. The problem is that you don't know how to bring them to the surface. In this chapter we will discuss some useful techniques that will help you break through blank-page paralysis and capitalize on your best thinking.

Associating the word *invention* with computers may suggest to some people that computer programs will give students ideas that can form the basis for writing. This is not true. Even interactive computer programs that are specifically designed to stimulate invention (see the Appendix) do not come up with new ideas. Writers have to use prewriting techniques to discover ideas for themselves. Word processing programs can help writers record, store, and revise their ideas and enable them to move easily from invention activities to drafting. You may already know the invention techniques we discuss in this chapter. What we will show you is how word processors can be used systematically to record the results of invention activities and then to organize this prewriting into first drafts of papers.

This chapter provides you with a range of prewriting activities. In any given activity the prewriting strategies you use will depend upon the specifications of the assignment and your personal habits of mind. Strategies that work very well for one writer may not be helpful to another. As you read this chapter, think how you might apply the prewriting strategies to specific assignments, and note the strategies that seem particularly useful.

Throughout this chapter we will assume that all prewriting is typed on a word processor and stored in a textfile. Depending upon your hardware and software, you may end up dividing your prewriting among more than one textfile. After we have presented the basic prewriting activities, we will discuss ways to organize your prewriting, either within a single textfile or split up among several different textfiles.

ASSIGNMENT SPECIFICATIONS

A useful way to begin prewriting is with a one-page entry in which you record the specifications of the assignment. After a heading that gives your name, the course title, and the paper's due date, type in the assignment. This is especially important when the original assignment was given orally or written on the board. It will protect you from misinterpreting the nature of the assignment as you proceed. Underline any key words that are crucial to your aim and purpose in writing.

Now record the length of the assignment, and consider the audience for whom the piece is intended. Are you writing to a general audience of educated readers or to a more specific group? What knowledge, attitudes, and beliefs do you and your audience have in common? Does your audience have any special needs? What impact will your writing have on your audience? How will it inform, influence, change, or call them to action? These questions will lead you to the next area of concern: the pattern of development. Does the assignment require you to use a particular strategy or plan (for example, compare and contrast or cause and effect), or do you have the freedom to determine your own organizational format? Try to come up with a few possible plans at the outset. This will help you to understand the assignment better and will suggest how you should approach further prewriting activities.

Next, speculate on the content of the paper and the sources of information you will draw on as you write. For some assignments your own experiences and personal knowledge will provide the source. For other assignments you will need to collect information from readings and other outside sources.

To complete the assignment page, reread what you have written up to this point and try to formulate a preliminary statement describing your goals. For example, "In this paper I will support the psychological theory that first-born children tend to share common personality characteristics."

A sample printout of an assignment page is shown in Figure 2.

Colin Siegele
Foundations of Writing
Prof. Brody

Assignment #2
Due: Feb. 15

ASSIGNMENT:

The traditional nuclear family consisting of father, mother, and child is no longer the prescribed normative structure in the United States. Can other family structures replace this father-mother-child triad or should it remain the primary family type? In a three-page paper, draw on your own experiences and give your predictions about the future of the nuclear family.

LENGTH:

About 750 words

AUDIENCE:

Other first-year college students. This audience will have first-hand knowledge of the topic through their own family experiences and their observations of other families. My peers may not share all my beliefs, but I hope to show that I have a reasonable argument.

POSSIBLE PLANS FOR DEVELOPMENT:

I might compare and contrast (families my parents grew up in vs. families today vs. families in the future) or use cause and effect to show how societal forces, such as divorce and late marriages, lead us to view the nuclear family in a new way.

PRELIMINARY GOALS:

In this paper I will try to convince my peers that the nuclear family will continue to decline in popularity unless people take specific measures to change traditional family roles.

SOURCES:

My own knowledge and experience.

Figure 2. Sample printout of an assignment page.

When you have typed and saved the assignment page, print a copy. If you have any questions about the requirements of the assignment and your intended method of approach, show the assignment sheet to your instructor. Some of the most common difficulties of college writers stem from misconstruing the assignment and drifting from it in the course of writing. The assignment page provides you with a compact, legible statement of your understanding of the task at hand. Take it to conferences with your instructor or to help sessions at your campus writing center.

INVENTING AND COLLECTING IDEAS

After you have clarified the assignment, the next step is to come up with material you can use in your first draft. First, you will want to tap your own knowledge and experience, and then, if the assignment requires it, you will need to consult readings and other outside sources. Prewriting techniques for bringing your ideas to the surface—brainstorming, clustering, freewriting, and journal writing—adapt quite well to the word processor.

Brainstorming and Clustering

Through a process of free association, brainstorming helps activate knowledge and ideas that are related to the assigned topic. The steps in this process are listed below:

BRAINSTORMING
1. Reread the assignment and come up with a target word, idea, or concept that is pivotal to the assignment. Center this word on the first line of a new page. 2. Double space and quickly list all the words and phrases the target word brings to mind. Leave three or four spaces between words, and triple space between lines. Give your imagination free rein; do not worry about sticking to the topic.

Figure 3 shows an excerpt from a brainstorming list based on the nuclear family assignment:

Nuclear family: father + mother + child(ren)

Extended family: grandparents, aunts, uncles, cousins

One-parent family: mother + kids; father + kids

Yuppies: husband and wife, one or no kids

Divorced family: stepparents, stepbrothers and -sisters

Adopted kids, foster kids

Homosexual family: gay or lesbian parents

Fifty percent of U.S. marriages end in divorce; increasing number of one-parent families

Traditional family: father works; mother is housekeeper and child rearer (stereotypes)

FIGURE 3. Excerpt from a brainstorming list.

Today * Most wives and mothers work; need day care and babysitters for children

* Women come home to housework and kids; they get tired out

* Some couples share housework and child rearing

Families are smaller today: 1 to 3 kids (China allows only 1 child per family)

FIGURE 3. (continued)

After you have covered several screens with words and ideas, you can begin to *cluster*, to link related words and phrases from your brainstorming list. Clustering shows you the relationships between your ideas and suggests organizational patterns for your writing. Follow these steps to cluster your brainstorming list:

CLUSTERING A BRAINSTORMING LIST

1. Save and then print out your brainstorming list. Lay out the pages on a surface so that you can see the entire list at once.
2. Read over the brainstorming list and look for similarities, patterns, and connections. Review the words and ideas by moving successively from one word to the next, or try to find interconnections by looking at the whole simultaneously. Jot notes in the margin to remind yourself of any patterns and connections that you see.
3. Return to the word processor and cluster the brainstorming list to reflect the patterns and connections you identified. Use the cut-and-paste function (see page 12) to bring together related ideas. Type in headings that describe the categories or patterns you use to cluster the material. Capitalize all letters in the heading so that they will stand out. In a category labeled "MISFITS" group any ideas that do not fit into other categories.
4. When you have clustered the brainstorming list according to one scheme, save the rearranged list under a new textfile name so that you can still access the original list. Using any other organizational plans that occur to you, repeat the clustering process and save each rearranged list under a new textfile name. When you have exhausted all possible plans, print out each of the clustered lists.

USING WORD PROCESSOR WINDOWS AND BUFFERS

If your word processor conveniently allows you to divide textfiles into subsections and then store the subsections in separate buffers or windows, this feature can make clustering much more efficient. Use a buffer or window for each category of information. Cluster by moving items from the brainstorming list to the windows or buffers. Then save the categorized sublists as separate files, or combine them into a single file.

The following figure shows two idea clusters from the brainstorming list we considered earlier:

TRADITIONAL FAMILIES

Nuclear family: father + mother + child(ren)

Extended family: grandparents, aunts, uncles, cousins

Traditional family: father works; mother is housekeeper and child rearer (stereotypes)

NEW TYPES OF FAMILIES

One-parent family: mother + kids; father + kids

Yuppies: husband and wife, one or no kids

Divorced family: stepparents, stepbrothers and -sisters

Homosexual family: gay or lesbian parents

Most wives and mothers work; need day care and babysitters for children

Women come home to housework and kids: they get tired out

Some couples share housework and child rearing

Families are smaller today: 1 to 3 kids (China allows only 1 child)

FIGURE 4. Excerpt from clustered brainstorming list.

Brainstorming at a word processor allows you to cluster the ideas on your list. You can use the cut-and-paste function to reorganize your list without having to recopy it as you would working with pen and paper. Since the clustering process is easier on the word processor, you will be more likely to try several clustering plans; thus, you will have various options from which to choose.

Focused Freewriting

Another way of generating material for your first draft is through focused freewriting. This technique helps you bring to the surface your ideas and past associations with a given topic by allowing you to follow *nonstop* a train of thought. Do not worry about making sense or using correct spelling and sentence structure. Your goal is to get down all you know about the assigned topic. Later, you will focus your freewriting further by selecting relevant and meaningful ideas and deciding what perspective emerges from your freewriting.

Freewriting works well on a word processor. By lowering the brightness control on the monitor, you can force yourself not to worry about correctness, because you cannot see the letters you are typing on the screen. Stephen Marcus and Sheriden Blau call this technique "invisible writing."* Invisible writing prevents you from rereading and correcting typos, misspellings, and other errors and thus frees you to concentrate on discovering ideas.

Continue freewriting until you have exhausted your supply of ideas. Then turn up the brightness control and read your work. At this point the word processor makes it easy for you to revise or add to key parts of your freewriting. Decide which ideas are meaningful, isolate them on the screen, and expand on them. When the most relevant ideas stand out, you can eliminate unnecessary material.

There are any number of ways to revise freewriting with the aid of a word processor. One method is as follows.

REVISING AND CLUSTERING FREEWRITING

1. Save a copy of the textfile that contains your freewriting. Then move the cursor to the top of the file and turn on the delete-block marker so that advancing the cursor will mark a block of text for deletion. With many word processors the text that is marked will be highlighted on the screen as the cursor advances.
2. Read through your freewriting on the computer screen, and pause when you find an idea that seems particularly relevant to the assigned topic. Position the cursor immediately before this idea and activate the block delete to erase the text that comes before this idea. Move the cursor to the end of the relevant idea and once again turn on the delete-block marker.
3. Move through your entire freewriting, saving relevant ideas and deleting irrelevant material. Rather than connected sentences, you will now have a list of ideas that pertain to the topic.
4. Move the cursor back to the top of the prewriting file, and read through the list. Now, use the cut-and-paste function to cluster related ideas as you did in your brainstorming

* Stephen Marcus and Sheridan Blau, "Not Seeing Is Relieving: Invisible Writing with Computers," *Educational Technology* 23 (4): 12–15.

list (see page 22). Group together in a category labeled "MISFITS" any ideas that seem relevant to the topic but do not fit into other categories.

5. Build a paragraph from each idea cluster by combining related phrases, expanding on individual phrases, adding new sentences, and providing transitions between ideas. In some cases, you may want to make a generalization based on a specific example that appeared in your freewriting. Type a topic sentence for the paragraph that states the main idea. Capitalize all letters in the topic sentence so that it stands out.

The steps we presented above will help you build rough paragraphs that center on the key ideas from your writing. You might choose to stop this activity at Step 4 and then combine this material with a brainstorming list. Or you might stop at Step 3 and then freewrite further in response to each of the ideas on your list. Adapt this process to your own needs and preferences.

Figure 5 shows an excerpt from a student's freewriting on the topic of the nuclear family. Remember that by its very nature freewriting is rough and disorganized. Following the initial freewriting is the student's attempt to identify and expand on some of the key ideas that emerged from the freewriting session (Figure 6) and then an excerpt from a clustered freewriting list (Figure 7).

Until I was eleven, I lived in a nuclear family. There was my mother, my father, my older brother Danny, and me. Then my parents got divorced. Dad and Dan moved to North Carolina, but I stayed in New York with my mom. So my nuclear family split into two one-parent families. But not for long. When I was thirteen, Mom remarried. Suddenly, I had a stepfather, two stepsisters, and a stepbrother—a family of six. My stepbrother was only five years old, and my stepsisters were both under ten, so after always being the baby of the family, I had three younger siblings to watch out for and help take care of. My dad never remarried and lives alone since Dan is in college now. My new family is much different from my first family. When we were little, my mom was a housewife. She cleaned our bedrooms, did our laundry, cooked all the meals, washed the dishes. After school, she was home waiting for us with a snack. She made sure that we got right to our homework and gave us any help with it that we needed. Today, things are different. Mom is a buyer for a department store. When she gets home from work, my stepdad, who teaches high school, already has dinner started, and I often help him. In general, I do a lot more around the house than I used to, and have had to take on more responsibility for my school work and my personal needs. My stepdad

FIGURE 5. Excerpt from focused freewriting.

also does other types of housework, and all three of us help take care of the younger kids.

I have very few friends who live in nuclear families. Most of their parents are divorced. My best friend lives alone with her mother and, like me, my roommate has a stepfather. I believe that a divorce often liberates a woman. Many of my mother's friends were homemakers until they split up from their husbands. Then they had to support themselves, so they resumed their careers or went back to school. It's very difficult for a woman to have a full-time job and be expected to clean the house, cook, and take care of the kids.

FIGURE 5. (continued)

Then my parents got divorced.

So my nuclear family split into two one-parent families.

Suddenly, I had a stepfather, two stepsisters, and a stepbrother—a family of six.

So after always being the baby of the family, I had three younger siblings to watch out for and help take care of.

My dad never remarried and lives alone since Dan is in college now.

My new family is much different from my first family.

When we were little, my mom was a housewife. She cleaned our bedrooms, did our laundry, cooked all the meals, washed the dishes. After school, she was home waiting for us with a snack. She made sure that we got right to our homework and gave us any help with it that we needed.

Today, things are different. Mom is a buyer for a department store.

When she gets home from work, my stepdad, who teaches high school, already has dinner started, and I often help him.

FIGURE 6. Excerpt from a list of selected freewriting ideas.

In general, I do a lot more around the house than I used to, and have had to take on more responsibility for my school work and my personal needs.

My stepdad also does other types of housework, and all three of us help take care of the younger kids.

I have very few friends who live in nuclear families. Most of their parents are divorced.

I believe that a divorce often liberates a woman. Many of my mother's friends were homemakers until they split up from their husbands. Then they had to support themselves, so they resumed their careers or went back to school.

It's very difficult for a woman to have a full-time job and be expected to clean the house, cook, and take care of the kids.

FIGURE 6. (continued)

FAMILIES ARE CHANGING

Then my parents got divorced.

So my nuclear family split into two one-parent families.

Suddenly, I had a stepfather, two stepsisters, and a stepbrother—a family of six.

My new family is much different from my first family.

I have very few friends who live in nuclear families. Most of their parents are divorced.

NEW FAMILY PATTERNS CHANGE THE LIVES OF MOTHERS

When we were little, my mom was a housewife. She cleaned our bedrooms, did our laundry, cooked all the meals, washed the dishes. After school, she was home waiting for us with a snack. She made sure that we got right to our homework and gave us any help with it that we needed.

FIGURE 7. Excerpt from clustered freewriting.

Today, things are different. Mom is a buyer for a department store.

I believe that a divorce often liberates a woman. Many of my mother's friends were homemakers until they split up from their husbands. Then they had to support themselves, so they resumed their careers or went back to school.

It's very difficult for a woman to have a full-time job and be expected to clean the house, cook, and take care of the kids.

NEW FAMILY PATTERNS CHANGE THE LIVES OF CHILDREN

So after always being the baby of the family, I had three younger siblings to watch out for and help take care of.

In general, I do a lot more around the house than I used to, and have had to take on more responsibility for my school work and my personal needs.

Figure 7. (continued)

Figure 8 shows a rough paragraph that the student developed from one of her freewriting idea clusters. Keep in mind that this is not yet polished writing.

OVERALL, CHANGES IN THE TRADITIONAL NUCLEAR HAVE BENEFITED WOMEN. The traditional role of housewife and mother kept women from having careers, since it's very difficult for a woman to have a full-time job and be expected to clean the house, cook, and take care of the kids. When women get divorced, however, they often become liberated. Many of my mother's friends were homemakers until they split up from their husbands. Then they had to support themselves, so they resumed their careers or went back to school. This pattern is certainly true for my family. When we were little, my mom was a housewife. She cleaned our bedrooms, did our laundry, cooked all the meals, washed the dishes. After school, she was home waiting for us with a snack. She made sure that we got right to our homework and gave us any help with it that we needed. Today, things are different.

Figure 8. Rough draft from an idea cluster.

At this stage, the writer's goal is to establish focus, not to produce a well-structured, grammatically correct piece of writing. Even from the standpoint of idea development, the paragraph in the example has flaws. For instance, it describes the situation of middle-class women but not necessarily that of working-class and poor women. Still, the student has come a long way toward identifying a perspective that she can develop more fully as she organizes and drafts her paper.

Journal Writing

A college teacher often asks students to record their reactions and responses to the course in a journal. Journals can take many forms. They can be daily or weekly chronicles of thoughts on a particular topic, records of observations of some phenomenon over time, reactions to assigned readings, or responses to particular questions posed by the instructor. Word processors work well in journal writing because they make it easy to expand an entry at a later date. If you are keeping your journal in a bound notebook, you may find it cumbersome to add or respond to thoughts you wrote down earlier. Textfile directory systems, on the other hand, make it easy to locate material within the journal, especially since some systems automatically assign a date to the files.

Heuristics

Another way to collect ideas for your papers is to use *heuristics*. Heuristics are systematic procedures writers use to explore their topics at the prewriting stage. A common heuristic you might use is asking *journalists' questions* (Who? What? When? Where? How? Why?) about the assigned topic. For the assignment that asks you to predict the future of the nuclear family, you might ask the journalists' questions and generate the following ideas:

USING JOURNALISTS' QUESTIONS

WHO?

- Nuclear family: mother, father, children
- Husband and wife without children
- One parent families
- Families enlarged and reduced from divorce
- Extended families
- Gay and lesbian families

WHAT?

- Nuclear family structure is no longer the norm.
- What is the definition of a family?
- People have to live together and share, but do they have to be related?

WHEN?

- Past: Nuclear families, many of which were rather large families, with husbands and wives in stereotypical sex roles
- Present: Fewer nuclear families, roles beginning to change
- Future: More nontraditional families; nuclear family members will have to assume new roles

WHERE?

- U.S. and Europe: nuclear families declining
- Asian countries (China): nuclear family is norm

WHY?

- Many marriages end in divorce
- Couples choosing to remain childless
- Women are pursuing careers

HOW?

- Nuclear family may continue to be a viable structure if husbands and wives assume less traditional roles

After you have recorded your responses to the journalists' questions in a textfile, scroll through the file and select the questions that led to the most promising responses. What patterns of development do these categories suggest? For example, the "When?" responses imply a chronologically ordered paper that compares and contrasts families in the past, present, and future. Use the word processor to organize your list of responses according to the pattern(s) you selected. Expand any ideas that seem incomplete, and revise them where necessary. If possible, try several different patterns, and save each version in a separate file.

Another systematic way to think about a subject is in terms of what are often called *"topics."* Topics represent lines of thought or patterns, such as definition, comparison/contrast, cause/effect, and evidence. If you examine your subject in terms of questions based on these topics, you will discover many useful ideas. Here are some questions you can use to generate ideas.

CLASSICAL TOPICS

TOPIC: DEFINITION

What is the nature of the subject you are writing about?
To what general category does it belong?
What is its function?

TOPIC: COMPARISON AND CONTRAST

Can you compare/contrast the subject to something else?
How many similarities/differences are there?

TOPIC: CAUSE AND EFFECT

What do you think are some possible causes or antecedents of the subject?
What will be its effects or consequences?

TOPIC: EVIDENCE

Can you recall any experts' opinions on the subject?
Are you aware of any statistics about it?
Have researchers studied the subject? What have the researchers found?

A third springboard for discovering ideas about a given subject is called *tagmemics.* This heuristic helps you view your subject from three perspectives that correspond to type, development, and context. The first defines your subject as a *particle,* or self-contained entity; the second describes it as a *wave,* or entity subject to change over time; the third depicts it as a *field,* or entity that is part of larger context or environment. With each of these perspectives in mind, you can devise a series of questions for probing your subject. Here are a list of questions a writer could use to explore the "family."

TAGMEMIC QUESTIONS

PARTICLE (Self-Contained, Stationary Entity)

What is a nuclear family? How would you define it? Describe it. What are its characteristics?

WAVE (An Entity That Changes over Time)

What is the history of the family? What were families like in the past? Are they different today? What will they be like in the future? Are changes in the family occurring rapidly or slowly? What are the effects of the changes?

FIELD (An Entity That Is Part of a Larger Context)

How is a family similar to or different from other groups of people? What characteristics do families share with other groups? How are they different?

As with other invention strategies, heuristics typically generate an unpatterned list of ideas that needs to be organized and revised. Scroll through your responses to heuristic questions and choose those that are most relevant to your topic. At this point you may wish to cluster related ideas using the procedure described on page 22. You may also choose to expand on these selected responses by freewriting.

If you use a particular heuristic regularly, set up a textfile that serves as a *template* for it. A template file contains a pattern that can organize material on a variety of topics. Into the template file type the list of questions or activities that make up the heuristic. When you want to explore a heuristic for your prewriting, simply load the template file into your word processor and answer the questions. Then save these questions and answers under a new textfile name so that the template file remains and can be called back.

COLLECTING IDEAS FROM READINGS

Invention strategies will enable you to bring to the surface what you already know about a given subject. At the same time, they will make you aware of all that you don't know. If there are gaps in your knowledge, tap other idea banks. For most college writing assignments, the most accessible sources of ideas are reading materials. The writing assignments you receive in college often require you to demonstrate academic learning in addition to or in place of general knowledge, experiences, or personal judgments. Professors expect you to formulate your own thesis or position on topics and issues, but they want you to support your view with evidence from textbooks, library books, reserve readings, and other reliable academic sources. For example, consider this modification of the assignment we considered above on the nuclear family:

> Over the past two decades there has been a dramatic increase in one-parent families in our society, but according to some sociologists, the two-parent nuclear family is still the preferred family structure. Attack or defend this notion in a three- to five-page paper. Draw on the articles you have read by Linton, Gough, and other sociologists.

This assignment requires you to draw on the written work of sociologists, not simply on your own experience. You will have to *read* articles or books, or both, *record* your comments and reactions to authors' key ideas, and *extract* bits of information that you can incorporate in your paper.

Just as a computer cannot invent ideas for you, it cannot understand reading sources. However, your word processor can help you record and organize material you gather from readings, as well as your comments and reactions to reading sources. In addition, strategies for word processing can help you become a more active and effective reader of academic prose.

Using the Word Processor to Record Your Comments and Reactions to Reading Sources

Reading is a two-way communication process between you and another writer. "Talk" directly to this writer in your mind and in your reading notes. At first you may have to make a conscious effort to read in this active way, especially if you have been a passive reader most of your life. In the following excerpt from a student's reading notes, note how she responds directly to the author's ideas and relates them to both her own opinions and the goals of the writing assignment:

"The nurturing female role is *socially* learned."
(Sally Linton, "Primate Studies and Sex Differences," p. 43)

This idea could be the main support for my position about changing male and female roles. A lot of these authors (Gough, Luepnitz) say the woman's role as child caretaker and homemaker is determined by society and the environment. It's *not* biologically determined. So why can't we help women unlearn the old role and learn a new one?

FIGURE 9. Excerpt from notes on a sociological article.*

Because it is often impractical to read sources in front of the word processor and type notes simultaneously, you may need to write out notes as you read and then transfer them to the word processor. Still, the advantages of electronic note taking will justify this extra step. Once you transfer your reading notes to a word processor, you can easily add to or modify entries, you can save a legible record of your work, and you can activate the directory system of your word processor to organize and keep track of the notes. You can also regroup notes and place related ideas together without recopying. In some ways, electronic note taking is similar to note taking on multiple index cards that you sort by category. The word processor's cut-and-paste function sorts the entires from your electronic notes more quickly, more economically, and more accurately than you would by hand. We will discuss this process in more detail in Chapter 3.

You can learn to read more assertively by asking certain strategic questions of your text. Three types of questions you can ask are (1) *content questions*, which explore the relationships between your own ideas and those of the author; (2) *analysis questions*, which enable you to look more closely at what the source means by taking the text apart; and (3) *synthesis questions*, which require you to connect the given material with other sources, books, and articles you have read. These three sets of questions are given below:

CONTENT QUESTIONS

1. Can I add any information to what the author is saying?
2. Do I agree with the author's view here? Do I disagree? Why?

* Sally Linton, "Primate Studies and Sex Differences," *Women: A Journal of Liberation* 1 (Summer 1970): 43–44.

3. Do I approve of the author's ideas? Do I disapprove? Why?
4. Am I satisfied with what the author has to say on the topic? Am I dissatisfied? Why?
5. How do I feel or what do I believe about this topic?
6. Do I have a question for the author? Have I answered any questions the author has raised?
7. Based on what the author has said, can I make a prediction?
8. Can I think of an example that illustrates the author's point? Can I think of a counterexample?
9. Have I had any personal experience relating to this topic?
10. Can I recall previous associations I've had with the topic or the author's views?
11. Can I make a generalization based on elements in common between the author's ideas and my own?
12. Can I think of an analogy to illustrate what the author is saying?

ANALYSIS QUESTIONS

1. What is the main, all-encompassing idea the author develops in the piece?
2. What is the primary plan the author uses to organize the entire piece? What secondary plans does the author use?
3. What is the author's format? What are the major organizational signals, such as introductory paragraphs, body paragraphs, headings, and conclusions?
4. Would the author's ideas be appropriate only for a special audience?
5. Does the intended audience have any special needs that the author is trying to meet?
6. Does the author's objective suggest that he or she has any goals other than presenting truth?
7. Are the author's goals intentionally hidden? If so, why?
8. Does the author assume the truth of things that may in fact be false?

9. Does the author assume that something that is true in a few cases will necessarily be true all the time?
10. Does the author's emphasis indicate a definite bias?
11. Does the author leave out any important ideas or facts that seem crucial to the issue?
12. Does the evidence presented clearly lead to the author's conclusion?
13. Is there an alternative conclusion that fits with the evidence as well as the author's conclusion does?

SYNTHESIS QUESTIONS

1. Does the source I am reading provide background for information in any other source?
2. Does it provide additional details about a point made in another source?
3. Does it provide support for the points made in any other source?
4. Does it contradict another source?
5. Are there points on which I can compare this source with other sources?
6. Can I contrast the ideas in this source with those in other sources?
7. What common threads run through the sources?

Type these three lists of questions and store each as a template file (see page 32). Each time you finish a reading, you can call up the template files and answer the guided reading questions. Skip questions that are irrelevant to the assignment. Then save the questions and your answers in a new textfile so that the original template files remain undisturbed.

Using the Word Processor to Extract Ideas from Reading Sources

In addition to storing in a prewriting textfile your responses to content, analysis, and synthesis questions, you can also store selected bits of reading material you plan to incorporate in your paper. Three strategies you can use for extracting ideas from reading sources are *direct quoting, paraphrasing,* and *summarizing.*

Direct Quoting: When you type in a direct quotation, reproduce the author's words *exactly* and place them within quotation marks. Identify the source by recording the appropriate documentary information: (1) the author's full name, (2) the title of the source, and (3) the facts of publication. Do not assume that the reader of your paper will understand a quotation you have taken out of context. Think about your audience's needs. If your reader should have background information in order to understand the quotation, include a paraphrase or summary of the context. Recording direct quotations on your word processor has a distinct advantage over writing your notes by hand. Once you have typed the quotations and their documentation into a prewriting file, you can transfer them electronically to the draft of the paper without retyping or recopying them.

Paraphrasing: A second useful strategy for recording ideas from reading is paraphrasing. Paraphrasing is the process of presenting someone else's ideas in your own words. The key is to retain the *exact* meaning of the original, using different words and rearranging the ideas. The following steps will help you accomplish this objective:

PARAPHRASING STEPS

1. Type the sentence or passage you wish to paraphrase. Then use the cut-and-paste function to produce a duplicate of the material immediately below the original.
2. On one copy of the sentence or passage, change the order of the phrases, clauses, or "idea units" in the sentence so that the material takes on a new pattern while still retaining its original meaning.
3. Substitute synonyms for words in the original wherever possible. Do not repeat more than three of the original words in a row.
4. Compare the paraphrase to the original, checking to see that you have reworded the idea sufficiently to call it your own but have retained its original meaning. For difficult sentences you may choose to duplicate the original several times over in order to try alternative paraphrases.
5. Record documentary information (author and page number) immediately after the paraphrase.

Summarizing: Here your primary goal is to make the original shorter without changing its meaning. Retain the main ideas, but leave out details and minor examples. Depending on the length of the passage you are summarizing, you can use several or all of the following strategies:

SUMMARIZING STEPS
1. Annotate the original text to delete redundancy and unimportant detail. Eliminate paragraphs, sentences, or parts of sentences, as you see fit. Mark these deletions with asterisks, and retain the thesis or topic sentence. Type the remaining material onto the screen. 2. Move the thesis or topic sentence so that it comes before all the other material. 3. Paraphrase the sentences on the screen. 4. Form a coherent paragraph or a number of paragraphs, by changing the order of sentences, combining and subdividing sentences, and providing transitions. 5. Record documentary information (author and page number) immediately after the summary.

Both paraphrasing and summarizing involve rewording and reorganizing segments of the original until you arrive at something that captures the idea of the original in language that you can call your own. A word processor is well suited to this task. Once you have relevant sections of the original source on the screen, you can substitute, delete, reorder, and add until you have a good paraphrase or summary. This process is much more laborious with pen and paper since you must recopy all the material several times over to get good results. Notice in the following examples how the student moves from the original sentence to an adequate paraphrase in several stages:

PARAPHRASING AN ACADEMIC SOURCE*

The family was made desirable by the early human combination of prolonged child care with the need for hunting with weapons over large terrains. The sexual division of labor on which it was based grew out of a rudimentary pre-human division between male defense and female child care (Gough 770).

* Kathleen Gough, "The Origin of the Family," *The Journal of Marriage and the Family* 33 (November 1971): 760–70.

The family was made desirable by the early human combination of prolonged child care with the need for hunting with weapons over large terrains. The sexual division of labor on which it was based grew out of a rudimentary pre-human division between male defense and female child care (Gough 770).

FIGURE 10. Example of duplicating source material.

The family was made desirable by the early human combination of prolonged child care with the need for hunting with weapons over large terrains. The sexual division of labor on which it was based grew out of a rudimentary pre-human division between male defense and female child care (Gough 770).

A rudimentary pre-human division between male defense and female child care gave rise to the sexual division of labor on which the family was based. The early human combination of prolonged child care with the need for hunting with weapons over large terrains made the family desirable (Gough 770).

FIGURE 11. Example of reordering basic idea units.

The family was made desirable by the early human combination of prolonged child care with the need for hunting with weapons over large terrains. The sexual division of labor on which it was based grew out of a rudimentary pre-human division between male defense and female child care (Gough 770).

Simple pre-human sex roles that cast females as child rearers and males as protectors led to sex-based labor in the human family. Because humans needed to hunt far from home but children needed care at home for several years after birth, the family structure, based on a hunter and a caretaker, was successful (Gough 770).

FIGURE 12. Example of substituting synonyms.

The family was made desirable by the early human combination of prolonged child care with the need for hunting with weapons over large terrains. The sexual division of labor on which it was based grew out of a rudimentary pre-human division between male defense and female child care (Gough 770).

Simple primate societies, in which females were child rearers and males were protectors, set a pattern for human families that evolved later. Since hunting took humans far from home, but human children needed care for the first few years of their lives, a family structure based on a hunter and a caretaker was successful (Gough 770).

FIGURE 13. Example of final adjustments to a paraphrase.

Note that the student is careful to retain the author's name and page number in order to document the paraphrase. For each source you should also keep complete documentary information (author, title, facts of publication) so that when you draft your paper, you can copy the information for a list of references.

When you have recorded relevant ideas from your readings, you can cluster them according to the procedure we describe on page 24.

ORGANIZING PREWRITING TEXTFILES

When you work on short papers with only a few screens of prewriting, you probably will have little trouble locating ideas in your notes and bringing relevant parts of your notes together as you draft your paper. If, however, you are working on longer papers with extensive prewriting, you need a systematic way to order your notes for efficient recall as you draft your papers. When you plan your prewriting activities, you should also decide how many textfiles—one,several, or many—you will use to store your prewriting. Of course, this decision depends not only upon the scope of the assignment but also upon the capabilities of your word processor. Certain elegant word processing programs allow you to arrange your notes into various textfiles that you can view simultaneously on the screen and rearrange, recombine, and revise at will. Features such as windows, splitscreens, and text buffers make these manipulations possible (see page 12). If your word processor has these features, you may find it easy and advantageous to subdivide your notes into separate textfiles. For instance, if you cluster your freewriting as we describe on page 24, you may want to save each major cluster in a separate file. Since these blocks will likely develop into separate sections or paragraphs, they will best serve your needs as free-standing units that you can organize in your first draft. You will certainly find it easier to access each block directly, rather than scrolling through a long file of blocks in search of the right one.

Use only as many prewriting files as your machine can handle efficiently. Some word processors handle multiple files better than others do. If you are working with more than four or five textfiles, it may help to establish a directory of textfiles that lists the name and briefly describes the content of each one. Such directories save a great deal of time on long research projects. Perhaps the greatest danger of using many separate prewriting files is that you may be more likely to forget to save them. Make sure you save all the files you have created or changed at the end of each work session.

Even if your word processor does not have capabilities for viewing and revising several files at once, you may want to divide your prewriting among several files. In this case you merely revise each file separately and then merge them when you draft your paper. This is not as quick or efficient a process as using windows or split screens, but it gets the job done. If your microcomputer has a modest internal memory (64K or less), use several files for extensive prewriting notes. Computers with relatively small internal memories may slow down considerably when they are required to handle long files.

For assignments that are not long, you may choose to keep all your prewriting in one file. When you cluster your prewriting in a single file, make the subsections stand out. For instance, you might center and capitalize all subsection titles and highlight the subdivision boundary with a line of dashes or asterisks; use new page commands to separate subsections; or preface long files with a table of contents that lists the subsections. When you use clear organizational divisions, you can find information easily as you scroll through the file.

REVIEWING PREWRITING FILES

Teachers want to guide students at all stages of the composing process, but they are thwarted by illegible handwriting at the stage of invention. Do your prewriting activities at the word processor and your instructor will be able to assist you. Print out a double- or even triple-spaced version of your prewriting file(s) so that there will be plenty of room for your instructor's comments.

A final word:

BACK UP PREWRITING FILES JUST AS YOU WOULD BACK UP DRAFT FILES

EXERCISE 2. COMBINING INVENTION STRATEGIES: BRAINSTORMING AND FREEWRITING

Choose a topic you will have to write on in the near future, one you are already interested in or about which you know nothing.

1. Follow the brainstorming procedure on page 20 to produce a list of words and phrases related to your topic. Brainstorm for a minimum of ten minutes. Cluster your brainstorming list according to the procedure on page 22. Save the textfile.
2. Freewrite on your topic for at least fifteen minutes according to the procedure on page 23. Revise and cluster your freewriting following the procedure on page 24. Save the textfile.
3. Print out both your clustered brainstorming and your clustered freewriting. Compare the two lists, noting categories that overlap or points of conflict. Come up with a new clustering plan that encompasses both lists.

4. Merge the two textfiles into a single file. Revise the list according to the new clustering plan by combining categories from the two lists and creating entirely new categories if necessary. Save the new textfile.
5. Print out the combined clustered list. If your instructor wants you to go further, you can develop a rough draft from this list by following the procedures in Chapter 3.

THREE FOCUSING AND ORGANIZING

In this chapter we will explain how the word processor can help you organize ideas in your prewriting textfile, develop a sharp focus, and create a structural framework for the first draft of your paper. Even though you may have clustered your invention notes to group related ideas together, these clusters may be disconnected and fragmentary. In addition, they may be divided among several different textfiles. At this point you need to identify an organizational pattern for your paper and to arrange your notes according to this pattern. This framework will later guide you through the first draft of your paper. Students who are working from handwritten prewriting notes often bypass this part of the writing process because it involves recopying large sections of prewriting notes. With a word processor, focusing and organizing activities are no longer laborious and burdensome.

CLUSTERING

In Chapter 2 we explained how to cluster your invention notes so that related ideas come together in labeled categories or rough paragraphs. Although we describe a distinct clustering strategy for each type of invention notes, all these strategies have the same basic result: They help you identify the key ideas in your notes. Now you will develop the structure of your essay from these key ideas. Cluster your invention notes if you have not done so thus far. (We give step-by-step directions for clustering on pages 22–25.) If your notes are already clustered, verify that each cluster is labeled with a word, phrase, or topic sentence that conveys the cluster's key idea. Capitalize all letters in each label so that the labels stand out. Label one section "MISFITS" for any ideas that do not fit with other clusters.

Note that if you used several different invention strategies, you will have a different set of idea clusters for each strategy. Later in this chapter we will discuss combining these clusters.

Below is an excerpt from a set of clustered notes. Recall that at the beginning of the invention process we discussed an *assignment page* on which you record the basic requirements of the assignment and define goals for your paper. Such an assignment page describing the writing task is shown in Figure 14.

FIGURE 14. An assignment page.

Annie E. Smith | Assignment #1
Composition 101 | Due: Feb. 15
Prof. Penner

ASSIGNMENT:

Draw on your own experiences and the readings we have done in class to evaluate the role of grades in higher education.

LENGTH:

About 750 words

AUDIENCE:

Other first-year college students. This audience will have extensive personal experiences with grades.

POSSIBLE PLANS FOR DEVELOPMENT:

Compare and contrast (good vs. bad aspects of grades); cause and effect (how grades affect education)

FIGURE 14. (continued)

PRELIMINARY GOAL:

In this paper I will try to convince my peers that even though grades can affect some students negatively, they are a necessary evil.

SOURCES:

My own experience plus the following articles: selection from The Community of Scholars, by Paul Goodman "A Young Person's Guide to the Grading System," by Jerry Farber and "A Grading Experience," by Kenneth Boulding.*

GRADES CAN INHIBIT LEARNING

In high school I was reluctant to take courses that I didn't think I could get good grades in. I tried taking French my freshman year, but after I got a C I decided to drop languages because my grade point average and class rank would suffer if I continued. I now have forgotten the little French I learned. In fact, I don't know anything about foreign languages. This cuts me off from majors that require languages. In college I avoid biology courses because I am afraid that my grades will suffer if I try to compete with the pre-med students who regularly take those courses.

Grades turn education into a "game." After each semester, you forget what you just studied, last semester's game, and go on to the next round. All that counts in this game is how you do on the test, not what you retain (Farber 67).

Grades just cause students to focus on their grade point averages. Education takes a back seat to the all-important grades.

FIGURE 15. Example of clustered notes from freewriting.

* Paul Goodman, *Compulsory Mis-education and the Community of Scholars* (New York: Vintage, 1964); Jerry Farber, "A Young Person's Guide to the Grading System," in *The Student as Nigger* (New York: Pocket Books, 1970); Kenneth Boulding, "A Grading Experience." *Technology Review* (October 1979): 8-ff.

GRADE INFLATION:

My parents had to work hard for C's and were happy to get them when they went to college in the late 1940s. In some of their courses, over half the class would fail. Professors maintained strict standards and did not bend when students had trouble meeting these standards.

In the 1980s a C is a disappointing grade. And if a lot of students do poorly on a test, the professor usually raises all the grades. You know that you won't have to work hard to get a C.

I would think that grade inflation would hurt the best students. It is hard for anyone to stand out from the pack when grades are inflated.

FIGURE 15. (continued)

FOCUSING ON KEY IDEAS

As you work to establish a structure for your paper, you need to think about how your central ideas interrelate. You can focus better on these central ideas if you separate them from the details in the rest of your notes. Recall that for each idea cluster in your notes, you wrote a capitalized heading that identified the cluster's key idea. Now, by collecting these headings, you can construct a *key-idea file* that includes only the important ideas and omits the details. Before you create a key-idea file, save the entire file of invention notes so that it will not be lost. Then scroll through your invention notes and delete all material except the capitalized idea cluster headings. *Save these headings under a new file name so that the original invention notes remain intact.*

Below is a sample key idea file for the assignment on grades in college:

GRADES PROMOTE MEDIOCRITY RATHER THAN EXCELLENCE

GRADES GIVE STUDENTS A REALISTIC PICTURE OF THEIR OWN PROGRESS AND APTITUDE

GRADES CAN INHIBIT LEARNING

GRADE INFLATION

UNIVERSITIES NEED ACADEMIC STANDARDS

GRADES ARE NOT THE BEST WAY OF MEASURING LEARNING

GRADES ARE GOOD MOTIVATORS FOR STUDENTS

GRADES ARE A USEFUL YARDSTICK OF PROGRESS FOR TEACHERS AND STUDENTS

GRADES HELP ASSURE THAT DESERVING AND COMPETENT PEOPLE GET THE MOST REWARDING AND RESPONSIBLE JOBS

GRADES ENCOURAGE CHEATING

GRADES ARE NEEDED TO HELP ADMINISTER COLLEGES

FIGURE 16. Excerpt from a key-idea file.

GRADES LET STUDENTS KNOW THEIR STRENGTHS AND WEAKNESSES

GRADES DISCOURAGE INDEPENDENT LEARNING

GRADES HELP INSTRUCTORS AND ADVISERS KNOW WHICH STUDENTS NEED EXTRA HELP

GRADES PROMOTE FEAR AND ANXIETY

GRADES ARE A FAIR WAY OF DISTRIBUTING REWARDS AND PRIVILEGES

GRADES MAKE STUDENTS COMPETE RATHER THAN COOPERATE

GRADES DISTRACT EMPLOYERS FROM OTHER ABILITIES THAT COLLEGE GRADUATES MAY POSSESS

GRADES MAKE STUDENTS FOCUS ON INDIVIDUAL COURSES RATHER THAN ON THEIR OVERALL EDUCATIONAL GROWTH

GRADES MAKE COLLEGES INTO MERE SCREENING AGENCIES FOR EMPLOYERS

GRADES SERVE AS "INFORMATION ECONOMIZERS"

GRADES HELP GUIDE STUDENTS' WORK

FIGURE 16. (continued)

If you have stored your invention notes in more than one textfile, merge all the headings into a single key-idea file.

REEVALUATING PREWRITING GOALS: A PRELIMINARY THESIS

The material you use from your invention notes should be consistent with your goals for the paper. To compare your statement of goals with your invention notes, print and read the key-idea file and the assignment page.

Ask yourself whether the material in the bulk of the prewriting file is consistent with these goals. If not, you may need to revise your goals or generate new material. Often you will find that your prewriting has taken you in a direction you did not initially anticipate. There is nothing wrong with this. Prewriting activities are meant to generate new thoughts. Often your best thinking is stimulated by the process of clustering and reorganizing your notes. Now, you need to select the parts of your prewriting that are both interesting and in line with the specifications of the assignment.

At this point you may want to revise your goals further to come up with a *preliminary thesis.* A thesis is a compact statement of the main idea that a writer will demonstrate or prove. Many college writing assignments call for papers that present theses and then support them with evidence and logic. If your assignment requires a thesis, reword your goal statement. State the main point you want to make in the paper. Then try to narrow this point by assigning limits to it, qualifying it, and sharpening your assertion. Take, for example, the preliminary goals statement for the assignment on the family in Chapter 2:

> In this paper I will try to convince my peers that the nuclear family will continue to decline in popularity unless people take specific measures to change traditional family roles.

By eliminating the statement of intention and by qualifying and specifying the main point, the writer soon arrives at the following preliminary thesis:

> For the traditional nuclear family to survive in the next century, men and women must be willing to share parenting, home responsibilities, and breadwinning duties.

If you intend to develop a preliminary thesis statement, return to the word processor, locate the assignment page, and proceed as follows.

CONVERTING A STATEMENT OF GOALS TO A PRELIMINARY THESIS

1. Use your word processor's copy function to produce a duplicate of your preliminary goals statement. Place this duplicate immediately after the original statement and change the label from "PRELIMINARY GOAL" to "PRELIMINARY THESIS."
2. Revise this statement until it expresses the main idea you want to develop in your paper. You may need to delete parts of the original, add new material, or even depart entirely from the preliminary goals.

Consider the following example from the assignment on the role of grades in college. We have excerpted from the assignment page the preliminary goal and shown how the student changed this goal into a preliminary thesis. Notice that the student has retained the basic idea from the preliminary goal, but she has made it more specific.

PRELIMINARY GOAL:

In this paper, I will try to convince my peers that even though grades can affect some students negatively, they are a necessary evil.

PRELIMINARY THESIS:

In this paper, I will try to convince my peers that though grades can affect some students negatively, they are a necessary evil.

FIGURE 17. Example of deletion.

PRELIMINARY GOAL:

In this paper, I will try to convince my peers that even though grades can affect some students negatively, they are a necessary evil.

PRELIMINARY THESIS:

Although grades can distract some students from learning, they are a necessary evil.

FIGURE 18. Example of substitution.

PRELIMINARY GOAL:

In this paper, I will try to convince my peers that even though grades can affect some students negatively, they are a necessary evil.

PRELIMINARY THESIS:

Although grades can distract some students from learning, they provide the motivation that many students need to succeed in college.

FIGURE 19. Example of addition.

When you are satisfied with your preliminary thesis, save the file containing the assignment page so that you retain both the statements of your goals and your thesis.

ORDERING YOUR IDEAS

Up to this point you have separated your notes into idea clusters, refined your writer's goals, and, if appropriate, written a preliminary thesis. The next step is to establish an organizational framework that presents your ideas in a logical order and that highlights their interconnections. Papers proceed in a linear fashion from a beginning to end, but your idea clusters may expand in a more or less random order, and the links between them may not be clear. Physically grouping the cluster headings is one way of identifying these links. This is a job that your word processor can do with ease when it moves the headings in your key-idea file.

Using the Assignment to Generate a Plan

You will soon find that you need to organize your notes according to some basic pattern. There are a number of patterns you can use. First, see if the assignment itself suggests any particular structure. Consider the following assignment from a psychology course:

> The articles we have discussed in class presented conflicting opinions on the extent to which heredity on the one hand and environment on the other

determine our personalities. In a 1,000-word essay, survey the range of opinions presented in the articles we covered and then defend your own opinion on the heredity versus environment issue.

The assignment suggests that the paper should have two basic parts: one section in which you survey the range of opinions on the heredity versus environment issue and another in which you defend your own view on this issue. It makes sense to survey the experts' opinions before you center in on your own. Thus, you might begin by giving some logical order to the views of the experts. Then you might gather all material that explains your own position and place it after the experts' opinions. You could present the evidence that indicates that the environment is the key factor, follow with the evidence that heredity is most important, and then consider compromises between these two positions. As you can see from this example, the organizational pattern you use often depends upon the assignment and the particular material you generate at the prewriting stage.

In various academic disciplines, there are set organizational formats that specify the order in which you should present your material. A good example of this is the psychology research report, which includes an abstract, an introductory section, an explanation of the experimental method, a description of the experimental results, and a discussion of the results. Make sure you are aware of any standard organizational formats that are specific to the discipline, course, or instructor. If a particular format applies, number your prewriting material to conform to it.

ORGANIZATIONAL PLAN TEMPLATES

Note that if you regularly use a particular organizational format, you might store the outline for this format in a textfile and use it as a template for the writing plan. See page 32 for more information about templates.

Choosing an Organizational Pattern

If no particular pattern is suggested by the assignment, reread your key-idea file to see if you can group any of the idea units. Look for relationships among the ideas and try to arrange them in patterns. Think in terms of the topics we discussed in Chapter 2 (page 31) and in terms of other basic patterns of arrangement.

YOU CAN ARRANGE IDEA UNITS BY SHOWING HOW CERTAIN IDEAS

- Describe other ideas in terms of attributes, specifics, or characteristics.
- Compare and/or contrast with other ideas.
- Serve as the causes or antecedents, or effects or consequences of other ideas.
- Are evidence or support (views of experts, facts, examples, statistics, research, experiments, and so on) for other ideas.
- Constitute a definition.
- Describe a process.
- Show a chronology, sequence, or logical progression.
- Show a spatial relationship.
- Are either more or less important than other ideas.
- Are generalizations for which other ideas are particulars.
- Are either more or less obvious than other ideas.
- Are parts, classifications, or divisions of other ideas.
- Can encompass other ideas.
- Constitute a statement for which other ideas are a response.
- Constitute a question for which other ideas are an answer.
- Constitute a problem for which other ideas are a solution.
- Constitute a remark for which other ideas are a reply.

Consider how you might group invention notes for the assignment on college grades. Review the key-idea file shown on pages 47–48. Since the file is for the most part a list of the advantages and disadvantages of grades, you could organize your paper to contrast these advantages and disadvantages as we see in Figures 20 and 21 on the next page.

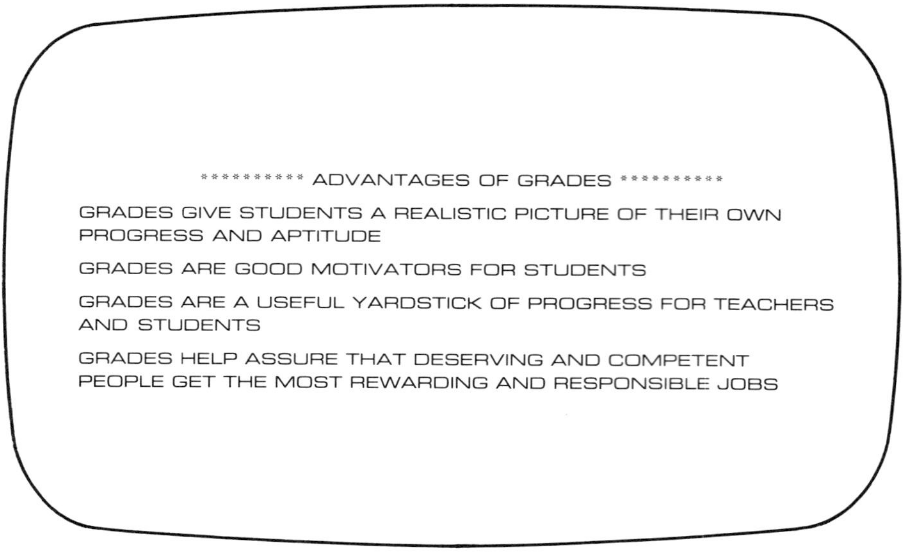

FIGURE 20. Key-idea file excerpt 1.

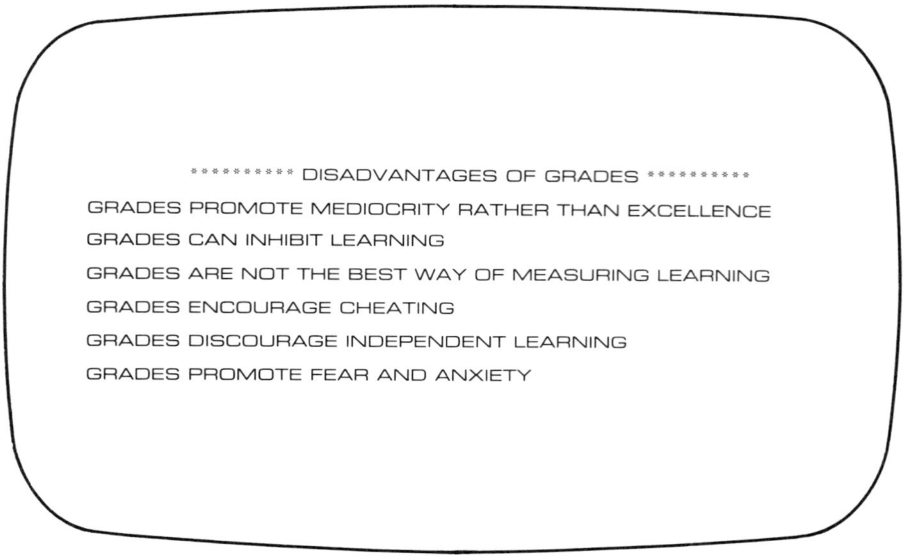

FIGURE 21. Key-idea file excerpt 2.

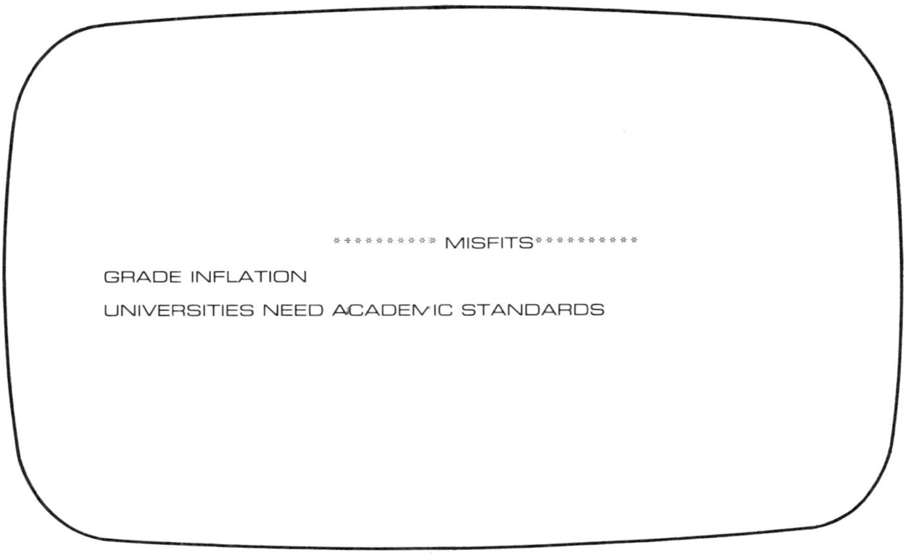

FIGURE 22. Key-idea file excerpt 3.

Notice that we have added organizational signals to indicate the pattern you are using. Make these organizational signals stand out by using obvious dividers, such as the asterisks in the example, that will catch your eye as you scroll through the file. The "MISFITS" section is for ideas that do not fit in with the pattern you have chosen. You may eventually use this material at the drafting stages even though it does not readily fit in now with your overall plan.

Developing an Argument

Writers often think of planning as the process of developing an *argument*. In the broad sense argument does not imply a combative stance but merely a reasoned explanation of a particular position. Some thesis statements imply directly the manner in which the supporting argument might be developed. For instance, assume that you are writing an essay in which you argue that grades motivate reluctant learners but at the same time prevent them from becoming independent learners. Clearly, this thesis implies an argument based on a cause-and-effect pattern. Other patterns of argumentation emerge from using different schemes. One such scheme describes one-, two-, and three-dimensional arguments. A one-dimensional argument presents a thesis and then lays out all the evidence that directly supports it. A two-dimensional argument presents and directly supports a thesis but also recognizes ideas that compete with the thesis and responds to these alternatives. Whereas a one-dimensional argument hammers away at a single thesis, a two-dimensional argument recognizes and accounts for exceptions to the thesis. A three-dimensional argument not only states a thesis and explores competing hypotheses but also tries to explain the relationship between the thesis and its competition. It shows that neither the one nor the other is complete in itself, that both interact with, modify, and perhaps even determine each other. Whether you intend to construct a one-, two-, or three-dimensional argument will to a great extent determine the way in which you sequence your prewriting notes. Other schemes for structuring arguments may also influence your organizational plan for writing.

Comparing Alternative Plans

Do not assume that the first organizational plan you come up with is the one on which you should base your paper. In most cases there will be several different plans you can use to pattern any set of key ideas. For instance, a cause-and-effect pattern could be used to organize material for the assignment on college grades: An initial section on the reasons why colleges stress grades might lead into a section that explains the effects of grades on education. Here is how the pattern would work:

********** WHY COLLEGES STRESS GRADES **********

UNIVERSITIES NEED ACADEMIC STANDARDS

GRADES ARE A USEFUL YARDSTICK OF PROGRESS FOR TEACHERS AND STUDENTS

GRADES HELP GUIDE STUDENTS' WORK

GRADES ARE NEEDED TO HELP ADMINISTER COLLEGES

GRADES HELP INSTRUCTORS AND ADVISERS KNOW WHICH STUDENTS NEED EXTRA HELP

********** HOW GRADES AFFECT EDUCATION **********

GRADES CAN INHIBIT LEARNING

GRADES ARE GOOD MOTIVATORS FOR STUDENTS

GRADES ENCOURAGE CHEATING

GRADES LET STUDENTS KNOW THEIR STRENGTHS AND WEAKNESSES

GRADES DISCOURAGE INDEPENDENT LEARNING

FIGURE 23. Excerpt from a reorganized key-idea file.

Since you can duplicate your key-idea file as many times as you want, you can experiment with possible organizational plans by making extra copies of your key-idea file and reordering them according to various patterns. Word processing has a clear advantage over working with handwritten prewriting notes because you can experiment without manually recopying substantial amounts of the material. Try several maps before you decide which one is best. Try to determine which plans seem most clear, logical, and effective. Think of your audience as you make this decision, since it is the audience that will need to comprehend and follow the plan. To remind yourself of the readers you address, study again your description of the audience on the assignment page at the beginning of your prewriting file.

After you have tried several organizational plans, review the one-page assignment and goals statement, and then decide which pattern works best for the material you have collected. Often you will base your papers on two or more organizational patterns. In any case, make sure the plan you choose will fit with the specifications of the assignment.

Rearranging Your Invention Notes to Fit Your Plan

When you select a suitable plan, print out a copy of the reordered key-idea file. Your next step is to reorganize your invention file(s) to fit this plan. Use either of the following techniques.

REORGANIZING INVENTION NOTES

1. If your invention notes are all in one file, move the idea clusters until they are in the same order as in the key-idea file. Then type the organizational signals from the key-idea file at the appropriate locations in the invention file. In essence, you are imposing a plan on the original invention file.
2. If your invention notes are in several different files, move the idea clusters from the invention files to the appropriate positions in the key-idea file. Depending on the characteristics of your word processor, you may use one of several techniques for swapping ideas clusters among files (see page 12). In essence, you are gathering the details from your invention notes to flesh out a plan in the key-idea file.

As we mentioned above, make the organizational signals stand out so that your pattern is clear. Include all your invention notes in the reorganized file, even the information that falls under the "MISFITS" heading. Do not eliminate these ideas from the file, as you may decide to use them later. Leave intact the assignment page with the statement of preliminary goals or preliminary thesis. When you are working with material from reading sources, make sure that author and page number appear after each idea.

Subdividing the Parts of Your Organizational Plan

After you have identified an overall plan for your paper and reorganized your invention notes according to this plan, you may see subpatterns within the major organizational divisions. For instance, consider the organizational plan on page 54, where the material on grades was divided into advantages and disadvantages. The cluster of ideas on the disadvantages might be subdivided into effects on students, effects on college as an institution, and effects on society as a whole. This pattern is reflected in the following example showing how a student subdivided her prewriting notes for the assignment on grades:

*************** DISADVANTAGES OF GRADES ***************

------------FOR STUDENTS-------------

GRADES CAN INHIBIT LEARNING

In high school I was reluctant to take courses that I didn't think I could get good grades in. I tried taking French my freshman year, but after I got a C I decided to drop languages because my grade point average and class rank would suffer if I continued. I now have forgotten the little French I learned. In fact, I don't know anything about foreign languages. This cuts me off from majors that require languages. In college I avoid biology courses because I am afraid that my grades will suffer if I try to compete with the pre-med students who regularly take those courses.

Grades turn education into a "game." After each semester, you forget what you just studied, last semester's game, and go on to the next round. All that counts in this game is how you do on the test, not what you retain (Farber 67).

Grades just cause students to focus on their grade point averages. Education takes a back seat to the all-important grades.

FIGURE 24. Excerpt from a reorganized invention notes.

GRADES PROMOTE FEAR AND ANXIETY

I have a friend who ended up in psychological counseling because of anxiety over grades.

Worrying about the grades keeps you from being able to show what you know.

Figure 24. (continued)

The student in the example could go on to subdivide categories further until she reached a level at which the material was no longer readily divisible. Another step would be to place the ideas within the subdivisions in a logical order. In general, the more information you have in your notes, the more frequently you will need to subdivide categories.

OUTLINING

Undoubtedly you have been taught in the past to *outline* ideas as a precursor to writing. Outlines differ from the structured notes we discussed earlier in that outlines are typically sparse; they show only the structure of the paper, usually without much detail. However, outlines do vary in degrees of specificity and format, depending on which methods you use. No matter how you outline, a word processor can help.

Why produce outlines? Outlines let you see the structure of your prewriting notes in a compact form, devoid of the details that can obscure form. A clustered prewriting file or set of files may be very lengthy and unwieldy if you have done a lot of prewriting. This is especially true for research papers. In these cases organizational patterns will be clearer to you if you outline your ideas before you write. Outlining makes the main ideas stand out.

Formal outlining involves categorizing ideas hierarchically to show their relative importance. The most important issues or the broadest generalizations are labeled with capitalized Roman numerals. The next most important pieces of information are grouped underneath the upper-level items and are labeled with capital letters. All the levels of embedding are shown below:

```
I.
  A.
    1.
      a.
        i.
```

You can produce an outline from your clustered and sequenced notes as follows:

PRODUCING AN OUTLINE

1. Load into the word processor the file of clustered and sequenced notes.
2. If you have not done so already, divide each idea cluster into subclusters as we show on page 58.
3. Label each major organizational signal with a Roman numeral. Label each major subdivision with a capital letter. Continue this process until each idea unit has been placed at an appropriate level in the hierarchy.
4. Make each idea unit as compact as possible. Wherever possible, edit paragraphs down to sentences, sentences down to phrases, and phrases down to key words. Identify the idea with as few words as possible.
5. From the assignment page at the top of the file, retain only the preliminary goal or, if you have one, the preliminary thesis. This statement of your general intentions should be at the top of the outline.

Figure 25 is an example of an outline for the paper on grades. Note the student has used an organizational plan that differs somewhat from the one we considered earlier.

FIGURE 25. Sample outline.

Preliminary goal: To describe both the positive and negative effects of grades on higher education.

- I. Effects of grades on colleges
  - A. Positive effects
    1. Maintain academic standards
    2. Identify students who need help
  - B. Negative effects
    1. Encourage cheating
    2. Inhibit learning (Farber 68; Goodman 255-256)
    3. Provide employment information rather than encourage learning
    4. Prevent students from seeing "the big picture" (Farber 67)
- II. Effects of grades on students
  - A. Positive effects
    1. Let you know where you stand
    2. Let you know where you need to improve
    3. Provide motivation
  - B. Negative effects
    1. Promote fear and anxiety
    2. Interfere with cooperation among students
    3. Discourage independent learning (Farber 69)
    4. Focus attention on GPAs, not learning
    5. Discourage poor test takers
- III. Effects of grades on society
  - A. Positive effects
    1. Serve as an "information economizer" (Boulding 83)
    2. Serve as a fair way to distribute rewards
    3. Assure competent people will assume important jobs in the society
  - B. Negative effects
    1. Promote mediocrity (Boulding 8)
    2. Orient employer to test results rather than performance

If you want the outline to be more concise than this example, you may need to edit individual items and leave only enough to identify the idea. You might also need to eliminate entirely the last level of embedding. Recall that outlining procedures vary in format and degree of detail. Modify the outlining procedure we have described so that it serves your own purposes. Note that we are using outlining as a technique for discovery, not as a means of abbreviating a paper you have already drafted. You may be accustomed to completing outlines after you are done writing, merely to fulfill the assignment requirement that an outline be handed in with the final paper. We maintain that outlining is most useful as you struggle to find meaning in the ideas you collected at the prewriting stage.

PARAGRAPHING

At this point, you may want to go one more step and divide the prewriting file into paragraphs. Some students find security in knowing what will appear in each paragraph before they begin to write. Others begin with a general idea map or outline and make decisions about paragraphing as they compose the first draft of the paper. Keep in mind that each paragraph should develop a clear thought and have a structural purpose with regard to the rest of the paper. We will discuss paragraphing in detail in Chapters 4 and 6.

KEEPING TRACK OF SOURCES

As you edit and reorder you prewriting file, do not lose track of the documentary information for reading sources. If you extract ideas from a single source and place them in various parts of the organizational pattern, make sure that each idea is labeled with the author's name. Failure to do this may lead to inaccurate documentation or even to plagiarism.

If your paper draws on reading sources, begin compiling a list of references. At the end of your revised prewriting file, start a new page and type the complete bibliographic information for each source you retained in the file. It may be easier to locate this information now rather than later in the writing process. To save time in the long run, enter the bibliographic information using the precise documentation style your assignment requires (MLA, APA, and so on). Take advantage of the word processor's editing capabilities to make sure that the reference entries are absolutely correct.

REVISING THE ORGANIZATIONAL PLAN

Print out the reordered version of your prewriting file. Read the printout carefully, and use the following list to check for organizational pitfalls:

ORGANIZATIONAL PITFALLS
• Is your revised prewriting file rearranged according to an organizational plan that your audience can reasonably detect? • Does the organization of your revised prewriting file match your outline? • Will all parts of the revised prewriting file develop the thesis and fulfill your goal? • Have you recorded documentary information for all the reading sources? • Have you backed up all prewriting files?

EXERCISE 3

1. Load into the word processor a set of invention notes for a topic you have been assigned in a course.
2. If you have not done so already, cluster the ideas according to the procedure on page 44. Provide headings for each idea cluster.
3. Create a key-idea file from the idea cluster headings, following the procedure described on pages 47–48.
4. Make two additional copies of the key-idea file. You may keep all three copies in the same file, or, if you wish, you may store them in three separate files.
5. From the list on page 53, pick three distinct patterns that could be used to organize your invention notes. Then, organize each copy of the key idea file according to a different plan. Type in clear organizational signals that show your plan.
6. Print out the three copies of the key-idea file. Be prepared to discuss the advantages and disadvantages of each of the three organizational plans.

FOUR
DRAFTING

We define drafting as the process of taking ideas from your prewriting file(s) and putting them into sentences and paragraphs that form a unified, coherent piece of writing. If you are working with handwritten notes, drafting requires you to copy all the prewriting material you want to use. If you have done your prewriting on a word processor, however, you can transfer sections of your prewriting directly to your draft without recopying them. You can also revise and add to these notes.

To begin work on your first draft, load your clustered and sequenced prewriting file into the word processor. This file is the product of the invention activities we described in Chapter 2 and the focusing and organizing activities we described in Chapter 3. You will revise this file further and add to it as you type the rough draft of your paper. Before you begin to draft your paper, reread the assignment page you composed when you started work on the paper (page 18) and revised when you organized your invention notes (page 48). Study the assignment and the statement on the assignment page about its audience. Keep these concerns in mind while you draft the paper.

A PLAN OF ATTACK

Some writers draft the introduction first because they want to present their ideas in order, paragraph by paragraph. Other writers prefer to know what the body of the essay will say before they compose the introduction or the conclusion. Each approach has its merits, but for our purposes here, we will first compose the body of the essay and then add the introductory and concluding paragraphs.

WORKING FROM A PREWRITING TEXTFILE

If you followed the procedures in Chapters 2 and 3, you will at this point have a prewriting file with idea clusters grouped according to your overall plan for the paper. Capitalized headings indicate both the key ideas of the clusters and the major and minor organizational divisions of the paper. You may also have expressed your plan in a formal outline. The file ends with the MISFITS section, the collection of prewriting ideas that did not fit conveniently into your organization pattern. You will also have an assignment page that includes a goals statement and, if appropriate, a thesis. You can now work directly from your prewriting file(s) as you draft your paper.

Prewriting Textfiles: A Case in Point

To illustrate the process of drafting, let's assume that you are assigned to write an analytical paper on issues raised by the Bernhard Goetz case. This case concerns an incident that occurred on December 22, 1984, in which Bernhard Goetz, a civilian, shot four black teenagers who allegedly tried to mug him in a New York City subway car. The event has sparked controversy on a range of issues involving civil rights, the legal system, and public safety. Your assignment page is shown in Figure 26.

Figure 26. An assignment page.

Elizabeth O'Donnell	Assignment #3
Composition 101	Due: Sept. 12
Prof. Kobre	

ASSIGNMENT:

According to various journalists and commentators, the Bernhard Goetz case has raised a number of serious societal issues. Write a 750-word paper in which you identify these issues and argue which of these issues you think are most important.

LENGTH:

About 750 words

AUDIENCE:

Other first-year college students. This audience will probably have heard or read newspaper accounts about the Goetz case. They may know the basic facts in the case, but they may not have thought about the issues involved.

POSSIBLE PLANS FOR DEVELOPMENT:

Description (describes three social issues the case raises); cause and effect (explain issues that resulted from the Goetz case); order of importance (order the issues from the least to the most important)

PRELIMINARY GOAL:

I will inform my audience about the various issues raised by the Goetz case and convince them that certain issues are more important than others.

PRELIMINARY THESIS:

Although a variety of issues have been raised by the case, the destruction of law and order is the most important one.

SOURCES:

My own experience and the following articles: "A Lesson Taught on the Subway," by Mike Royko, "The Fascination of the Goetz Case," by Ellen Goodman, and "The Subway Vigilante," by Manning Marable.*

FIGURE 26. (continued)

After you constructed the assignment page, you typed into your prewriting file your reactions and responses to the articles on the Goetz case. You also stored in the file direct quotations, paraphrases, and summaries of the authors' perspectives. To make sure that you had collected all the crucial facts about the case, you used the heuristic of "journalists' questions" described on pages 29–30. You also brainstormed a list of other

* Mike Royko, "A Victim Sees Goetz in a Different Perspective," *Los Angeles Times* 18 (Jan. 1985), part II: 5; Ellen Goodman, "Living in the Danger Zone," *Washington Post* 26 (Jan. 1985): A23; Marable Manning, "The Subway Vigilante," *The Times Monitor* 2, no. 15 (Jan. 30–Feb. 5) 1985, Ithaca, NY: 15.

social issues the Goetz case raised and then freewrote your own thoughts about them. As you completed each set of prewriting notes, you clustered related ideas together and typed headings in capitalized letters to signal the main ideas of the clusters. Next, you determined an overall plan for the paper based on the relationships among the main ideas expressed in these headings. Finally, you combined all your notes and organized them according to your plan. An excerpt from your sequenced notes is given in Figure 27.

Figure 27. Excerpt from organized prewriting notes.

* ISSUE: WHETHER GOETZ WAS UPHOLDING *
* OR UNDERMINING LAW AND ORDER *

THE VIGILANTE AS DEFENDER
OF LAW AND ORDER

There is no question that crime is rampant in the New York subways. I would not think of wearing my ring or gold on the subway. When I am in New York, I avoid riding the subway as much as possible.

If government cannot protect citizens from crime citizens must protect themselves (Royko).

Court system ineffective in dealing with street crime; criminals not punished frequently or severely enough (Royko).

Muggings will continue as long as muggers know they can get away with their crimes. Police rarely catch them. If citizens acted as Goetz did and took a more active role in preventing street crime, the muggers would realize that they could not victimize others without some risk to themselves. Citizens who want to preserve law and order must be willing to take upon themselves the responsibility for maintaining law and order.

There are just too few police and too many criminals in our major cities. Given this fact, the police simply cannot protect us in many situations.

As Goodman points out, people who have been mugged and menaced are "angry at troublemakers and angry at their hard-learned lessons in avoiding trouble . . . angry at giving up the skateboards and the public domain."

VIGILANTISM LEADS TO THE DECAY OF LAW AND ORDER

Vigilantism is often used to persecute people—for instance, the racist activities of the Ku Klux Klan. Vigilantism allows you to act on your prejudices. Who is to decide who in our society is "threatening"?

If we allow everyone the right to carry a gun and shoot down people perceived as threatening, we are moving away from democracy and toward fascism (Marable 15).

Criminals can disguise their motives by saying that they are acting as "vigilantes." Can Goetz prove that he was being mugged when he opened fire? Legitimizing "self-defense" of this type gives criminals an excuse for killing.

The Constitution protects Americans' right to a fair trial. When the vigilante becomes judge, jury, and executioner, this basic civil liberty is in jeopardy.

What about the "innocent bystander"? There were other people on the train besides Goetz and the muggers. Firing a gun in a confined space is dangerous to everyone in the vicinity. Innocent bystanders are more likely to get hurt when untrained civilians use guns. This threatens law and order rather than supporting it.

In the Old West, where men were allowed to carry guns openly, shootouts were relatively common. Why return to this state of affairs?

FIGURE 27. (continued)

CONVERTING IDEA CLUSTERS TO PARAGRAPHS SENTENCES AND

At this point, then, you have analyzed the idea units (your own thoughts as well as those of the authors you have read) and arranged them in collections or clusters grouped in turn according to certain plans (for example, comparison, contrast, cause and effect). The next step is to transform these clusters, first into paragraphs and then into sentences. In other words, you are ready to draft your paper. Proceed as follows:

FORMING PARAGRAPHS AND SENTENCES
1. Divide or combine idea clusters to form paragraphs. 2. Construct topic sentences. 3. Convert idea units to connected sentences.

Divide or Combine Idea Clusters to Form Paragraphs

Work sequentially through the idea clusters in the prewriting file. Study the given idea cluster and decide whether it would be appropriate to combine the idea units into a single paragraph or to construct two or more paragraphs. For example, you might convert the cluster "THE VIGILANTE AS DEFENDER OF LAW AND ORDER" to two paragraphs: one that explains the problem (government, courts, and police deal ineffectively with crime), and another that offers a solution (citizens should preserve law and order by acting as Goetz did). Depending on the length and other specifications of the assignment, however, you might want to combine the problem and the solution into a single paragraph. Keep in mind that idea clusters in your idea map will not always correspond one to one with paragraphs in the draft. Some large clusters may be divided into several paragraphs, and some small clusters may be combined into a single paragraph. As you form paragraphs, keep in mind that paragraphing should highlight your central ideas and help readers follow your train of thought. Your decisions about paragraphing may change at any point in the writing process.

When you divide an idea cluster into two paragraphs, use the cut-and-paste function of your word processor to separate the idea units into two groups. Insert carriage returns between the groups, and provide a capitalized heading that captures the key idea of each group. The original cluster heading may still work for one of the groups or it may be discarded altogether. Merging two clusters into a single paragraph will also entail moving idea units and rewriting the cluster heading.

Construct Topic Sentences

Each paragraph should develop a single central idea that is typically expressed in a *topic sentence*. If you are building a paragraph from an idea cluster, you can form a topic sentence around the idea cluster heading.

Take advantage of your word processor's revising capabilities to recast the sentence, several times if necessary, until the idea is clear. Here is an example of how a student revised her topic sentence.

THE VIGILANTE AS DEFENDER OF LAW AND ORDER

FIGURE 28. Idea cluster label.

The problem is that the police are unable to prevent street crime, and the solution is for people to become vigilantes who defend law and order on their own.

Because the legal system is so ineffective when dealing with crime, people have become angry enough to defend themselves by taking the law into their own hands and acting like vigilantes, as Goetz did.

Frustrated with the inability of the government, courts, and police to deal with crime, people like Goetz become vigilantes, self-appointed defenders of law and order.

FIGURE 29. Examples of topic sentence drafts.

Notice that the student retained all versions of her topic sentence as she worked on the screen. She can now choose among these possibilities and delete the irrelevant versions.

Although writers often place topic sentences at the beginning of paragraphs, this is not an absolute rule. The topic sentence can occur in other positions in the paragraph as well. In any case, it helps to compose the topic sentence first because it will force you to decide on the overall purpose of the other sentences in the paragraph. Keep in mind that not every paragraph has a single sentence that expresses the main idea. When expressing a complex idea, you may need a combination of several sentences or even all the sentences in the paragraph to capture the main point. In such a case, we say the topic sentence is inferred rather than stated explicitly.

Convert Idea Units to Connected Sentences

Turn to the other material in the idea cluster and decide on the operations you will use to combine idea units into paragraphs.

MOVING FROM IDEA UNITS TO SENTENCES
• Incorporate idea units as if they were complete sentences. • Combine units or embed one unit in another. • Break down long units into shorter ones. • Provide connective links that will show your reader the relationships between the various ideas.

As you perform these operations, be flexible. Do not strain to include material that does not fit easily into the paragraph. Combine sentences, and order sentences logically to develop the idea expressed in the topic sentence. Flesh out ideas that are partially developed so that sentences express complete thoughts. This process may involve adding, deleting, and rearranging certain thoughts, operations that your word processor is equipped to handle. In Figures 30 and 31, notice how the writer fleshes out the prewriting notes for the Goetz assignment.

THE VIGILANTE AS DEFENDER OF LAW AND ORDER

There is no question that crime is rampant in the New York subways. I would not think of wearing my ring or gold on the subway. When I am in New York, I avoid riding the subway as much as possible.

If government cannot protect citizens from crime, citizens must protect themselves (Royko).

Court system ineffective in dealing with street crime; criminals not punished frequently or severely enough (Royko).

Muggings will continue as long as muggers know they can get away with their crimes. Police rarely catch them. If citizens acted as Goetz did and took a more active role in preventing street crime, the muggers would realize that they could not victimize others without some risk to themselves. Citizens who want to preserve law and order must be willing to take upon themselves the responsibility for maintaining law and order.

There are just too few police and too many criminals in our major cities. Given this fact, the police simply cannot protect us in many situations.

FIGURE 30. Prewriting notes.

As Goodman points out, people who have been mugged and menaced are "angry at troublemakers and angry at their hard-learned lessons in avoiding trouble . . . angry at giving up the skateboards and the public domain."

FIGURE 30. (continued)

Frustrated with the inability of the government, courts, and police to deal with crime, people like Goetz become vigilantes, self-appointed defenders of law and order. The problem exists because muggers will continue to attack people as long as they know they can get away with their crimes. The police rarely catch muggers because there are too many criminals and too few police. When muggers are apprehended, as Royko points out, the court system is ineffective in dealing with them; they are not punished frequently or severely enough. Royko goes on to argue that if the government cannot protect citizens from crime, citizens must protect themselves. Increasing numbers of people agree with Royko. Goodman explains that these people, many of whom have been menaced and mugged, are angry, "angry at troublemakers and angry at their hard-learned lessons in avoiding trouble . . . angry at giving up the skateboards and the public domain." They want to be able to ride the subways without clutching their bags and hiding their rings and gold chains. They are so angry that they are willing to act as vigilantes and take upon themselves the responsibility for maintaining law and order. They are ready to follow in the footsteps of Bernhard Goetz.

FIGURE 31. First draft of fleshed-out prewriting notes.

AVOIDING WRITER'S BLOCK

A main objective of drafting is to flesh out your prewriting ideas, but you do not give too much attention to detail at this point. Avoid "writer's block," the condition where writers struggle interminably, seeking "right" words that just do not seem to come. Your objective at this stage should be to get as complete a draft as possible, but you should not get bogged down searching for the right word, particularly if this tends to frustrate you and interfere with the writing process. Remember that word processors make it very easy to revise and edit later. Do not be afraid to leave sentences partially developed if they give you trouble. If a word or phrase within a sentence does not come to you, leave an underlined blank in the sentence and add the missing word(s) when you revise. If your word processor makes it awkward to leave underlined blanks, as some do, use a string of question marks or another marker that will stand out. Remember that you will be able to use a spelling checker later to edit your paper. Below is a section of a first draft where the writer has left blanks to be filled in later:

One of the most common responses to the Goetz case immediately after the ???????????????? first occurred, was a feeling of satisfaction that at last a victim of street crime had struck back and ???????????????? his own rights. As Royko points out, many people feel that the judicial system protects the rights of the criminal at the expense of those of the victim. Royko thinks that despite the fact that Goetz ???????????????? the law, the alleged muggers still got what they had coming to them and were taught a valuable lesson.

FIGURE 32. Leaving blanks in first drafts.

Even though you should not get bogged down with details as you compose the first draft, do not refrain from making obvious corrections or revisions as you type. In general, it is easier to correct typos and other errors immediately after you make them since the cursor needs minor repositioning to get to the location of the error. You may spend a lot of time locating these errors after the draft is complete.

PARAGRAPH UNITY AND COHERENCE

As you develop paragraphs, make sure that they are unified and coherent. In a unified paragraph all sentences relate clearly to a single main idea. In a coherent paragraph repeated words and ideas, rewording of ideas, and transitional expressions (*also, for example, thus, similarly, consequently,* and so on) show the reader the logical links among the sentences. Using your word processor, you can easily eliminate material that has the wrong "fit" and add connectors that link ideas together. Look again at how a student developed a unified and coherent paragraph from material in the prewriting file. By comparing the following paragraph with the prewriting file on page 72, you can see which material the writer eliminated. See if you can find elements the writer used to make explicit the connections among the different ideas.

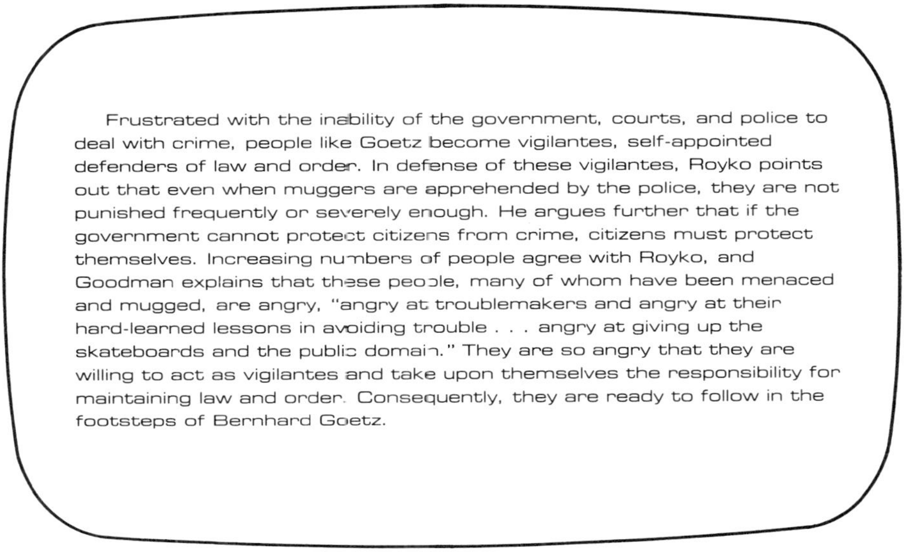

FIGURE 33. Example of paragraph unity and coherence.

When you have material that does not fit with the rest of the paragraph, use cut and paste to place this material into your MISFITS section. You can always change your mind and re-use ideas from the MISFITS section later. See Chapter 6 for more information on paragraph unity.

INTRODUCTIONS AND CONCLUSIONS

The function of the introductory paragraph(s) is to introduce the general topic area and present the thesis. You may wish to give your readers some background information about the subject and prepare them for what you will say about it. You might also inform your readers of your organizational plan and capture their interest.

The introduction should include a sentence or two that specifies your overall goal or thesis. Use the cut-and-paste function of your word processor to retrieve from the assignment page the goals statement or the thesis, and place it at the beginning of your draft. Read carefully through this statement or thesis to see if it expresses precisely what you accomplished in the body of your paper. If necessary, revise your goals statement or thesis.

Writers often place this general statement of their intentions at the very end of the introductory paragraph. The paragraph can begin in a number of ways, however. You might use one of the techniques listed below.

PAPER OPENERS
1. Quotation: Use an interesting quotation from one of your sources. 2. Question: Ask your reader a rhetorical question, for example, "Does the Goetz case indicate a regression to the gun-slinger mentality of the Old West?" 3. Anecdote or brief story: It happens every day. A gang of teenagers approach a defenseless subway rider and coerce him or her into giving them money. 4. Background information: On December 22, 1984, in a New York City subway car, Bernhard Goetz shot four black teenagers who, he thought, intended to mug him. 5. Generalization: Americans differ from almost all other nationalities in their strong belief in the right of citizens to bear arms. 6. Fact: Each year New York City police receive reports of thousands of muggings and robberies, but only a small percentage of these complaints ever lead to an arrest.

You may find a paper opener in the MISFITS section of the draft file. Scroll through this section and look for material that will both introduce the general topic and interest the reader. Use the cut-and-paste function to move any usable ideas to the beginning of the draft file. In the following example, the student has incorporated information from the MISFITS section of her prewriting notes as an opener.

According to William Safire, the word *vigilante* has two meanings. In the historical sense, the term refers to a vigilant citizenry, frontiersmen who worked together either to set up a peaceful society before law officials arrived on the scene or to maintain order when law officials were corrupt. In modern usage, however, *vigilante* refers to a person who takes control when he or she shouldn't and who uses methods of law enforcement that are uncalled for and out-of-date (9). By acting as a vigilante in the latter, negative sense of the term, Bernhard Goetz brought to our attention some serious issues, the most important of which is: Do private citizens have the right to bear and use arms for self-protection?

FIGURE 34. Information from the MISFITS section as an introduction.*

Finally, we move on to the last paragraph of the essay. Your concluding paragraph should do more than recapitulate the high points of the paragraphs that precede it. You should summarize your main points, but you should also use a rhetorical technique, such as (1) stressing the significance of your ideas, (2) predicting the consequences of your ideas, (3) calling your readers to action, and (4) ending with a question, anecdote, or quotation. Again, you may find material for the closing in the MISFITS section of your file.

If you are working on a very long assignment, the introduction and conclusion may extend beyond one paragraph. Recall from Chapter 3 that in certain situations, instructors may expect you to write according to a particular organizational format, and this format may dictate how introductions and conclusions are structured.

REVIEWING THE MISFITS SECTION

After you have finished drafting the body of your essay, move the cursor to the MISFITS section, where you stored ideas from your prewriting notes that you decided not to include in your draft. Scroll slowly through this section to see if any of the ideas might contribute to an existing paragraph or form the basis of a new one. Use your cut-and-paste function to insert any of these usable ideas into the body of the paper.

DIVIDING YOUR DRAFT AMONG SEVERAL TEXTFILES

Depending on the length of your paper, the capabilities of your word processing program, and your personal preferences, you will elect either to keep your draft in a single textfile or to keep various sections of it in different files. For papers under twenty pages in length you will probably

* William Safire, "Vigilante," *The New York Times Magazine* (February 10, 1985), 9–10.

decide to work on and store the entire draft in a single file. But as we mentioned earlier, some word processors have upper limits on the size of the textfiles they will handle, and many word processors are not designed to handle long files efficiently. Thus, you may choose to keep various parts of the first draft in separate files that you can work on one at a time. If you use more than one textfile, you may find it practical to print out a copy of each file as you finish with it, so that you can easily refer to the earlier parts of the paper as you compose. When you use several files as you draft, you will have to alter slightly the drafting procedures we have described above. For example, you would probably want to establish a separate MISFITS file and transfer from other files any idea units that do not fit into the clustering pattern you have chosen.

EXERCISE 4

Turn to page 67–68 and carefully reread the sample set of organized prewriting notes. Recall that we showed how a student developed a paragraph from the first idea cluster with the heading "THE VIGILANTE AS DEFENDER OF LAW AND ORDER." In this exercise, you will develop a paragraph from the ideas in the second cluster, "VIGILANTISM LEADS TO THE DECAY OF LAW AND ORDER." Use these steps to construct the paragraph:

1. Type on your word processor the idea cluster entitled "VIGILANTISM LEADS TO THE DECAY OF LAW AND ORDER" exactly as it appears on page 68.
2. Decide whether the cluster should form one or two paragraphs.
3. Construct a topic sentence for the paragraph.
4. Convert the idea units to connected sentences, using the techniques listed on page 69. Flesh out the ideas where necessary.
5. Compare your paragraph with those of other students in your class. What accounts for the differences you find?

FIVE
REVISING FOR FOCUS, DEVELOPMENT, AND ORGANIZATION

As we mentioned earlier, good writers do not march through lockstep stages of prewriting, drafting, revising, and editing. Stages often overlap. Reflect on your own writing process. As you compose a preliminary draft, do you ever pause, reread a portion of text, and cross out something that does not sound right? Or have you ever had an insight while revising a later draft and decided to insert the new idea? In a sense, each time you interrupt your flow of thought to reread and change what you have written, you are revising or editing. Most writers make changes of this sort in addition to revising and editing completed drafts.

Less able writers may revise and edit too much at the drafting stage. As they compose a first draft, instead of letting the thoughts flow and setting down all their ideas, they get "hung up" on concerns like choosing the right word, managing the correct spelling and punctuation, or even producing neat handwriting. When it comes to revising and editing completed drafts, however, many student writers do not know where to begin. Nor do they *want* to begin. They are often reluctant to change completed drafts because the process takes time and retyping requires extra work.

Enter word processing. Computers will motivate you to revise because they allow you to see your writing as fluid rather than fixed on the page. With one or two taps on your word processor keyboard, you can add, delete, substitute, or reorder text. Nevertheless, the word processor by itself will not make you a better reviser and editor. You need to develop your own strategies. The computer will facilitate the process, but it will not show you *how* to improve your written work.

We recognize that the ability to revise and edit effectively is not an inherent trait. Moreover, from experience we know that many college students have serious difficulties with these operations. Therefore, in this chapter and the two chapters that follow we will first offer you some strategies for revising and editing and then show you how the computer will enable you to put these strategies to work with ease.

For beginners we propose working in stages, starting with major revising concerns such as thesis creation, development, and organization, and later considering editing matters such as sentence structure, usage, punctuation, spelling, and mechanics. The reason for this progression is logical. There is no point in tinkering with commas and semicolons in rambling paragraphs that have no main ideas and make no sense. Work first on clear focus, development, organization, and coherence, then on awkward and incorrect sentences, and finally on errors in punctuation, spelling, and mechanics.

In this chapter we will concentrate on revising papers, first, for a clear focus, statement of thesis, and adequate development, and second, for effective organization and coherence. We will show you how your word processor can help you with five strategies for revising:

ORGANIZATIONAL REVISION STRATEGIES
1. Checking for focus and consistency 2. Adding, deleting, and reordering parts of the paper 3. Experimenting with alternative organizational plans 4. Highlighting transitional elements 5. Checking length

CHECKING FOR FOCUS AND CONSISTENCY

After you have completed a rough draft, set it aside for a day or more so that you can get some perspective on your work. When you return to your draft, do not reread it immediately. First, use the following procedure to *nutshell* the goal of your paper.

NUTSHELLING

1. Load the rough draft into your word processor and position the cursor at the very beginning of the paper.
2. Without rereading the draft, type a brief paragraph that summarizes the main point of the paper.
3. Compress this paragraph to a single sentence by deleting, rearranging, and, if necessary, adding information. Use the revising functions of your word processor to full advantage.

The resulting sentence should express, in a nutshell, what you feel your paper has accomplished. The following example illustrates this technique:

There are both costs and benefits to genetic engineering. Certain benefits, such as curing diseases and correcting defective genetic traits, outweigh the costs. The most important issue is whether or not the general public is knowledgable enough about genetic engineering. People should be informed about *all* applications of genetic engineering because in the long run, they are the ones who should decide under what conditions this technology will be used.

Some applications of genetic engineering promise benefits that are well worth the risks, but the public must become more aware of all genetic engineering's applications in order to make the right decisions about this new technology.

FIGURE 35. Example of nutshelling.

Now compare your nutshell sentence with your rough draft. The goal of this procedure is to see if your paper has a *focus:* a clear, sharply defined purpose consistent with the assignment and your intentions. Your paper should present a consistent perspective on the issue it addresses. You may find, however, that your paper departs from your initial intentions. This departure may start in the very first paragraph if your thesis statement differs from what you intended to say, or your ideas may shift gradually over the course of the paper.

Verify that the perspectives in your introduction and conclusion are consistent with your intended message. You can more readily make this comparison if you can see the introduction, conclusion, and nutshell at the same time. Do this by deleting all the text between the introduction and conclusion and then printing out what is left. With single spacing, the introduction, conclusion, and nutshell should fit on one page.

Now, read the nutshell sentence, introduction, and conclusion to see if the message is consistent throughout. If you detect inconsistencies, the paper either lacks a sustained focus or departs from your intended focus. The problem will necessitate major revision.

Try these procedures on the following example in Figure 36.

FIGURE 36. Comparing nutshell, introduction, and conclusion.*

Nutshell

Some applications of genetic engineering promise benefits that are well worth the risks, but the public must become more aware of all genetic engineering's applications so it can make the right decision about this new technology.

Introduction

In recent years we have made enormous advances in biology, primarily in the area of recombinant DNA and genetic engineering. Using modern technology, scientists have now discovered a way to control the genetic makeup of an individual; thus the term genetic engineering. As Carol Foote points out in her article, "Designing Better Humans," human genetic engineering has both benefits and dangers. However, I feel that the dangers outweigh the advantages. It concerns me that scientists are seriously suggesting that we make "better humans."

In brief, there are positive and negative applications of genetic engineering. I believe that this technology could improve medicine and food production. If we use it wisely, we

* Carol Foote, "Designing Better Humans," *Science Digest* (October 1982): 44.

Conclusion

can put an end to many diseases and help reduce world famine. If we use it unwisely, however, we may introduce new diseases, populate a "cloned" world, or possibly commit genocide.

Figure 36. (continued)

In this example, the nutshell and conclusion share a common perspective, that genetic engineering can be useful if applied intelligently. But what about the introduction? Notice that it attacks genetic engineering. Most likely, the writer began with a negative impression of genetic engineering but then shifted perspective while writing the paper. Because the act of writing stimulates new insights, writers often change their minds as they compose. Nevertheless, any variation in perspective must be adjusted in subsequent drafts so that the paper has a single, consistent focus.

Inconsistencies may have several different origins: (1) You write a paper that is consistent but does not express the message you intend; (2) you start off with a thesis that expresses your intention but you drift away from it as you compose subsequent paragraphs; (3) you start off with one intention expressed in your thesis, but you change your mind as you work and end the paper with a new position you discovered as you wrote. In all three cases you must examine the entire paper to determine how the shift took place. Printing out all the connecting sentences, a technique we will demonstrate later in this chapter (page 91), may help you to see how you drifted away from your original goal. When you revise the paper, you may need to eliminate whole chunks of irrelevant material, add more content, or reorder the paper according to a new organizational plan. As we will now show, word processors can help you accomplish all these tasks.

ADDING, DELETING, AND REORDERING PARTS OF THE PAPER

Among the tasks word processors do most efficiently are adding, deleting, or moving blocks of text. As we just mentioned, you may do these tasks to correct major inconsistencies, but you may perform these operations for other reasons as well. As you read through the draft of your paper, ask yourself the following questions (1) What should I add so that my audience can better follow my ideas? (2) What should I eliminate that does not contribute to my central focus? (3) What should I move that is out of place or needs to be grouped with similar material elsewhere in the paper?

We will first consider adding material to a draft. Figure 37 shows the first two paragraphs from a student's rough draft. The paper is weak and needs improvement. What do you think should be added to this section of the essay?

> Today, scientists are excited and optimistic about genetic engineering. It is supposed to be the answer to all of the world's problems. I disagree. This technology should not be used to improve the human species.
>
> I support using genetic engineering for some medical and agricultural research, but I think the research should be limited and closely monitored. We must guard against spreading any dangerous bacteria or viruses throughout the population. Alexander Hiam, author of *Sending DNA to War*, claims that the military is already developing genetic-engineering weapons, but we do not completely understand how these weapons will affect civilians. According to Hiam, had genetic engineering been developed during the Vietnam War, the military would have used it in the same way it used Agent Orange and other dangerous chemicals.

Figure 37. A first (rough) draft.*

This paper has several organizational problems. One of the most obvious is that the writer makes no attempt to explain genetic engineering to the audience. Perhaps the first task in revising should be to add, right after the introduction, a paragraph that defines genetic engineering. See how the paper reads with this addition:

> Today, scientists are excited and optimistic about genetic engineering. It is supposed to be the answer to all of the world's problems. I disagree. This technology should not be used to improve the human species.
>
> Genetic engineering involves at least three distinct processes: gene splicing, cloning, and selective breeding. Gene splicing and cloning are new techniques that scientists have successfully performed with lower animals and are contemplating using with humans. Gene splicing involves replacing parts of an organism's genetic structure in order to change its characteristics. For example, a defective gene that causes Down's syndrome could be replaced with a normal gene, thus eliminating the

* Alexander Hiam, "Sending DNA to War," *The Progressive* (October 1982): 19.

disorder. Cloning is making an exact copy of an organism by extracting some of its genetic material and using it to grow a new individual. Whereas in normal reproduction the offspring's genetic material is a combination of the genes of two parents, the clone obtains all its genes from one parent. The third genetic engineering technique, selective breeding, has been practiced for thousands of years with plants and animals and to some extent with humans. Selective breeding of humans requires that the parents be chosen carefully so that they will provide their offspring with genes for desirable traits.

FIGURE 38. Revision: definition paragraph added.

I support using genetic engineering for some medical and agricultural research, but I think the research should be limited and closely monitored. We must guard against spreading any dangerous bacteria or viruses throughout the population. Alexander Hiam, author of *Sending DNA to War*, claims that the military is already developing genetic-engineering weapons, but we do not completely understand how these weapons will affect civilians. According to Hiam, had genetic engineering been developed during the Vietnam War, the military would have used it in the same way it used Agent Orange and other dangerous chemicals.

FIGURE 38. (continued)

Whenever you add or delete a major section of your paper, take care that the new draft makes sense and conforms to your organizational plan. Read the new draft from beginning to end to make sure that it shows improvement.

EXPERIMENTING WITH ALTERNATIVE ORGANIZATIONAL PLANS

Some writing assignments specify particular organizational structures, for example, "Compare and contrast the authors' perspectives on . . ." Others expect the writer to select an organizational plan that suits the assignment, the reading sources, and his or her ideas on the topic. Sometimes you may not be able to identify the best plan *before* you write, but as you compose the first draft, you may discover it through trial and error. As you work on the draft, you will find yourself rethinking your ideas or seeing the material in a new light. By the time you finish the draft you may have discovered a new organizational plan, or you may have decided that the plan you began with is not adequate. In some cases, then, you might need to go through one or more drafts before you settle on a framework for the paper. You will recall that in Chapter 3 we presented a number of organizational plans. You can check that list on page 53.

As we mentioned above, many students are reluctant to revise the organization of their papers because this work is so time consuming and potentially risky. However, word processors make it relatively easy to try out various organizational plans and compare the results before you commit yourself to any one plan.

Figures 39 and 40 show how a word processor helps a writer with organizational revisions. An excerpt from the body of a first draft appears in Figure 39 and a second draft appears in Figure 40. The annotations on the second draft indicate revisions the student writer has made. Read the first draft carefully and try to figure out the organizational weaknesses. Then, as you read the second draft, look for places where the student corrected these organizational weaknesses. Finally, compare the revision to the first draft. The writing assignment is as follows:

> Write a short paper in which you weigh the pros and cons of genetic engineering. Draw on material from the reserve readings to support your views.

Note that the sample is not a complete paper, only a excerpt from the body of a paper.

FIGURE 39. Excerpt from a first draft.*

Views on Genetic Engineering

1st ¶ Harvard scientist Bernard Davis points out that genetic engineering can eliminate certain hereditary diseases such as Down's syndrome and Tay-Sacs disease (1280). By using recombinant DNA technology to alter

* Davis, Bernard. "Prospects for Genetic Intervention in Man." *Science* 171 (1970): 1279–83; Foote, Carol A. "Designing Better Humans." *Science Digest* (October 1982): 44; Huxley, Aldous. *Brave New World*. New York: Bantam Books, 1958; King, Jonathan. "New Genetic Technology: Prospects and Hazards." *Technology Review* (February 1980): 57–65; Nahas, Gabriel. "Genetic Meddling" in *Faith and Science in an Unjust World*, edited by Roger L. Shinn. Philadelphia: Fortress Press, 1980, 281–82.

the reproductive cells of individuals who carry genes for these diseases, scientists can prevent carriers' children and all later generations from developing the diseases. Thus, genetic engineering could possibly preserve the best and eliminate the worst human genetic characteristics. Davis also suggests that we might clone human beings to preserve the genes of individuals who make particularly significant contributions to society (1282).

2nd ¶

Foote summarizes the view of two genetic engineering experts, James Bonner and Robert Sinsheimer. Geneticist James Bonner argues that humans, like all other species, must continue to evolve to avoid extinction. Bonner supports a system of selective breeding that would allow only individuals who have the most desirable genetic characteristics to reproduce. Through this process, Bonner hopes we will develop the means to cope better with environmental and social problems that threaten our species. On the other hand, Sinsheimer points out that we can't know for sure what genetic characteristics will be needed in the future and thus shouldn't restrict the human gene pool intentionally. He also maintains that humans are not wise enough to decide what genes we may need in the future.

3rd ¶

Biologist Jonathan King also worries that we may not make the right decisions about what genes we will need in the future. For example, King points out that the sickle cell trait thought to be a disadvantage in Western culture is needed in central Africa because it provides a resistance to malaria (64). Before we eliminate genes that seem to be undesirable, we must be sure that they have no positive functions. But King does point out that we might be able to wipe out certain

Figure 39. (continued)

hereditary diseases through genetic engineering (60).

4th ¶ Scientist Gabriel Nahas questions whether humans have the wisdom to determine what genes are best. Instead, he favors trusting the results of millions of years of evolution and letting things develop naturally.

5th ¶ In his classic novel Brave New World Aldous Huxley demonstrates how genetic engineering could be used to enslave the world's entire population. In the futuristic society Huxley envisions, each person is genetically preprogrammed for a particular role. The society is orderly and stable but at the expense of freedom and individuality.

Figure 39. (continued)

Figure 40. Excerpt from a second draft.

Genetic Engineering: Pros and Cons

Add sentence to signal plan

From ¶ 2

From ¶ 1

From ¶ 1 and 3

Advocates of human genetic engineering maintain that through this process we can make major improvements that will benefit humanity. Geneticist James Bonner argues that humans, like all other species, must continue to evolve to avoid extinction (Foote). Bonner supports a system of selective breeding that would allow only individuals who have the most desirable genetic characteristics to reproduce. Through this process, Bonner hopes we will develop the means to cope better with environmental and social problems that threaten our species. Another suggestion is that we might clone human beings to preserve the genes of individuals who make particularly significant contributions to society (Davis 1282). Other scientists point out that genetic engineering could be used to eliminate certain hereditary diseases such as Down's syndrome and Tay-Sachs disease (King 60; Davis 1280). By using recombinant

From ¶ 1 — DNA technology to alter the reproductive cells of individuals who carry genes for these diseases, scientists can prevent carriers' children, and all later generations, from developing the disease (Davis 1280). Thus, genetic engineering could preserve the best and eliminate the worst human genetic characteristics.

Add concluding sentence

Add sentence to signal plan — Critics of human genetic engineering focus on the potential for error and abuse. Sinsheimer (Foote) and King (64) point out that we can't know for sure what genetic characteristics will be needed in the future and thus shouldn't restrict the human gene pool intentionally. For example, King points out that the sickle cell trait thought to be a disadvantage in Western culture is needed in central Africa because it provides a resistance to malaria (64). Before we eliminate genes that seem to be undesirable, we must be sure that they have no positive functions. Both Sinsheimer and Nahas question whether humans have the wisdom to determine what genes are best. Instead, they favor trusting the results of millions of years of evolution. In addition, human genetic engineering procedures can be abused by ill-intentioned people. In his classic novel Brave New World Aldous Huxley demonstrates how genetic engineering could be used to enslave the world's entire population. In the futuristic society Huxley envisions, each person is genetically preprogrammed for a particular role. The society is orderly and stable but at the expense of freedom and individuality. Thus, through either benign ignorance or evil intent, human genetic engineering may have disastrous consequences.

From ¶ 2 and 3

From ¶ 3

From ¶2 and 4

From ¶ 5

Add concluding sentence

FIGURE 40. (continued)

The first draft seems weak because the writer has organized the material of several authors by devoting each paragraph to a single source. When we look at the paragraphs as a unit, they seem disjointed and in places repetitious. At least one paragraph is far too short. Moreover, the writer's purpose is unclear. What does she want to accomplish by presenting these authors' views? Organizing by author can lead to structural weaknesses, but many students find it convenient to plan first drafts this way, particularly when the source material is complex. They work with one source at a time to avoid getting confused. This can be an appropriate technique for a first draft, but it will often necessitate careful organizational revision.

You probably observed that in the second version of the paper the writer uses many of the sentences from the first draft, but she groups all the advantages of human genetic engineering in one paragraph and all the disadvantages in another. This sets up a pattern that encourages the reader to weigh the pros and cons, which is what the assignment asks for. In the revised draft the writer adds little new material. The additions consist only of topic sentences and transitions that link together sentences according to the new organizational plan.

Once the student writer had decided to try a new organizational plan, the word processor made it relatively easy for her to move from the first to the second draft. Using the cut-and-paste operation, she grouped together advantages of genetic engineering in one paragraph and disadvantages in another. When two authors mentioned the same advantage or disadvantage, she used a single sentence to express their ideas. Finally, she added transitions and provided topic and concluding sentences for both paragraphs.

Word processors make it easy for you to regroup material from your first draft according to any number of organizational plans: time order, comparison and contrast, cause and effect, description, statement and response, definition, process, and so on. In our sample paper the writer uses comparison and contrast in the second draft since this pattern fits most clearly with the topic statement. But notice that statement and response might work as well. The writer could begin each paragraph with the statement of an advocate for genetic engineering and then give an opponent's response. Thus, she could use the word processor to produce a third draft according to the statement and response pattern and then compare it to the two earlier drafts. Word processing opens up more room for experimenting with organizational patterns than is practical with pencils and typewriters.

When you reorganize a draft using one or more alternative plans, make sure that you save the original draft as well as the revision(s). Print the drafts and compare them to determine which is best. Save all drafts in case you change your mind and decide to return to a plan that you rejected earlier.

HIGHLIGHTING TRANSITIONAL ELEMENTS

A major goal of organizational revision is to make sure that your reader can readily identify your organizational plan. You can give your reader clear signals if you use the first and last sentences in paragraphs to indicate the logical connections that establish an organizational pattern. The terms *topic sentence, transition sentence,* and *signpost* are often used to describe these signals. Such sentences, particularly topic sentences, not only weld together the ideas in the body of the paper but also make explicit links between ideas in the body and the thesis statement. They therefore provide the reader with a skeletal framework for the entire paper. Experienced readers will automatically look to these connecting sentences if they have difficulty following a writer's thoughts.

Because connecting sentences are so important in establishing your organizational plan, you should reread carefully the first and last sentences of each paragraph as you revise. Separate these sentences and look at them in isolation from the rest of the paper. Word processors make it very easy for you to do this. Just follow the steps listed below:

ISOLATING CONNECTING SENTENCES

1. Delete as a block all sentences in the introduction except for the thesis.
2. Step through the paper and delete as a block all sentences in each body paragraph except for the first and last. Insert a divider, such as a line of dashes, between each paragraph.
3. Delete the entire conclusion.
4. Print this skeletal framework. If your printing operation necessitates saving the file, make sure you do not erase the file containing the complete draft.

For drafts up to ten pages, this whole process should not take more than several minutes.

Isolating the connecting sentences highlights organizational problems that are not so obvious when the sentences are in context. Consider the example in Figure 41, which isolates a thesis statement and connecting sentences from a short paper on genetic engineering.

FIGURE 41. First version: isolating thesis and connecting sentences.

Thesis

The disadvantages of human genetic engineering far outweigh the advantages.

Changing the DNA structure of an organism can develop different characteristics.

Cloning is the exact copying of someone's genetic structure.

Connecting sentences

Foote's article contains various attitudes toward genetic engineering.

Huxley implies that genetic engineering will necessarily have these effects on society.

Harvard biologist Bernard Davis has published widely on the topic of genetic engineering.

Splicing genes can lead to unforeseen consequences.

FIGURE 41. (continued)

Looking at the connecting sentences in isolation, would you say that the paper has organizational difficulties? Notice that none of these sentences has an obvious connection to the thesis. In addition, the links between the paragraphs are not clear. Most likely, the writer has an organizational plan in mind, but she is not conveying this plan to the reader. Clearly, the connecting sentences need to accomplish more than they do in this draft.

In Figure 42, a revised version, the connecting sentences work more effectively.

FIGURE 42. Revised version: isolating thesis and connecting sentences.

Thesis

The disadvantages of human genetic engineering far outweigh the advantages.

Connecting Sentences

Human genetic engineering involves at least three distinct processes: cloning, gene splicing, and selective breeding.

Consequently, these various techniques of altering human genetic structure are all within the reach of modern science.

All three genetic engineering processes are dangerous to human society.

Thus, any one of the three methods of human genetic engineering may threaten the very nature of our society's political and social structure.

Despite the obvious dangers, some prominent scientists support human genetic engineering.

Clearly, arguments of genetic engineering proponents do not stand up under close scrutiny.

FIGURE 42. (continued)

The connecting sentences in this example signal the paper's organizational plan. The reader can see that the body of the paper will first define human genetic engineering, then show the problems with this technology, and finally examine and refute the views of proponents for genetic engineering. The connecting sentences now function as they should.

In Figure 43 we have isolated the connecting sentences in a short student paper. As you read through this example, what problems do you see?

FIGURE 43. Example: isolating thesis and connecting sentences.

Thesis

In no way should scientists alter the human species through genetic engineering.

Connecting Sentences

Some scientists have suggested creating a superhuman.

Thus, the superhuman concept is dangerous to our entire society.

A miscalculation with human genetic engineering could eliminate traits from the gene pool that we actually need.

We may not be able to retrieve human genes once they have disappeared from the gene pool.

Nature is held together by a complex interaction of plants and animals.

Changing the genetic structure of even the smallest plant or animal could disrupt the balance of nature.

FIGURE 43. (continued)

From an overview of the connecting sentences, it appears that the third paragraph does not suit the rest of the paper. It describes the overall effects of genetic engineering on the natural environment, but it does not focus on human genetic engineering. If the whole paragraph makes no reference to human application, it should be eliminated from the paper. This can be done at the word processor with a few key strokes. You can then print out the new version of the paper and see whether you need to make any transitional adjustments to cover the deleted paragraph.

CHECKING LENGTH

Most spelling checkers have a word-count feature that will tally the total number of words in your paper. Use this feature to see if your rough draft conforms to the length specifications given by the assignment.

EXERCISE 5

Load into the word processor a rough draft of one of your current writing projects. Check for focus and organization by performing the following operations:

1. Check for consistency by using the nutshelling technique described on pages 80–83. Is your nutshell sentence consistent with the perspective in your introduction and conclusion? Get the opinion of another student in your class.
2. Reread the list of organizational plans in Chapter 3 (page 53). Identify the plan(s) you adopted to organize your rough draft, whether it appears on the list or not. Select from this list a plan that is different from the one you used originally but is appropriate for your topic. Rearrange your paper according to this new pattern, being careful not to erase from your disk the original draft. Print out both versions. Which version is more effective? Why? Get the opinion of another student in your class.
3. Isolate the transitional elements in your rough draft by using the procedure described on page 91. Do the sentences serve as effective links between paragraphs and between the thesis and other parts of the paper? Get the opinion of another student in your class.

SIX
REVISING PARAGRAPHS

After you have analyzed the focus and development of your entire rough draft, you can review the focus and development of each paragraph in that draft. You can treat individual paragraphs with more confidence now that you have better control of your whole piece. In Chapter 4 we explained how writers can use the word processor to transform prewriting notes into paragraphs. In this chapter we will show you how to revise and refine paragraphs and make them more cohesive and coherent. Once again, an important consideration is your audience. As you look at each paragraph, ask yourself how you have helped your readers to determine your focus and follow your train of thought. Check that you have provided them with topic sentences and clear connections between your ideas.

TOPIC SENTENCES

A topic sentence is the generalized statement of a paragraph's main idea. It provides the reader with a framework for understanding the details in the rest of the paragraph. When it functions properly, the topic sentence makes it easy for the reader to comprehend and remember the paragraph's main idea. The topic sentence often comes first in the paragraph. Readers commonly expect that the first sentence in each paragraph will let them know in general what the paragraph will be about. There is no rule, however, about where the topic sentence should occur. Other positions within the paragraph provide suitable opportunities. Even when the topic sentence occupies the middle or the end of the paragraph, it can still tie together the other sentences. Occasionally, the topic sentence may be only implied rather than stated explicitly. Consider the following example where the topic sentence is implied:

> The Buddha is said to have achieved spiritual enlightenment through meditation and fasting. Similar procedures, however, are used to prepare for divine inspiration in religions the world over. This fact has implications for how one might view the development of religion in various cultures. Indeed, this aspect of the religious experience may be a direct response to man's universal physiological characteristics. People the world over share common experiences as a consequence of being members of the same species. It seems reasonable that they might interpret these experiences the same way.

The first sentence of the paragraph tells how the Buddha acquired spirtual enlightenment. The remaining sentences, however, discuss the religious experience of a much larger population: religious people throughout the world. The final sentence presents part of the paragraph's main idea: People everywhere have the same interpretation of certain experiences. Thus, we could say that the paragraph has the following unstated topic sentence:

> Human beings everywhere share certain experiences that they interpret as having religious significance.

To judge the effectiveness of topic sentences, whether they occur at the beginning, middle, or end of the paragraph or are implied rather than stated outright, first isolate the topic sentence from the rest of the paragraph. Then determine whether or not the topic sentence performs its role successfully. By viewing the topic sentence in isolation and then reading the paragraph without the topic sentence, you can better judge if it ties together the details for your audience. Use your word processor to check and, if necessary, adjust topic sentences according to the following procedure. Apply this procedure to all paragraphs *except the introduction and conclusion.*

REVISING TOPIC SENTENCES
1. Isolate the topic sentence. 2. Analyze the topic sentence's effectiveness. If the topic sentence is weak, revise it.

3. Revise other sentences in the paragraph to fit with the new topic sentence.
4. Revise paragraphs that have no topic sentences, either stated or implied.

Isolate the Topic Sentence

First, separate the topic sentence from the rest of the paragraph. Remember that the topic sentence is not necessarily the first sentence in the paragraph, although the initial position is common. Use the following steps:

ISOLATING TOPIC SENTENCES

1. Scroll through the paragraph, searching for the topic sentence. When you find it, place several asterisks both before and after it.
2. If you are unable to find a topic sentence, reread the paragraph to see if a topic sentence is implied. If one is implied, draft a version of the topic sentence *in capital letters* on the line immediately before the paragraph. If none is implied, type several question marks immediately before the paragraph.

Notice in the following example how the student marked the topic sentence.

***** According to Mehrabian, a third type of nonverbal communication is changes in body movements.***** Facial expressions, scratching, hand, arm, and leg movements are examples. Speakers who frequently move their heads or limbs unveil a fidgity, uninterested attitude towards their listeners. Changes in people's body movements also indicate how anxious they are in social situations. For example, listeners who constantly shift in their chairs convey to speakers that they are either bored or anxious. As people speak, if they lean toward their listeners, they show they are feeling positive. If listeners nod their heads in agreement, they are showing that they respond positively to the speakers' words.

FIGURE 44. Example of an identified topic sentence.*

Analyze the Topic Sentence's Effectiveness and Revise an Ineffective Topic Sentence

After you have identified a topic sentence, either explicit or implied, consider whether or not it ties together the other sentences in the paragraph.

ANALYZING THE EFFECTIVENESS OF TOPIC SENTENCES

1. Reread the entire paragraph except for the topic sentence itself.
2. Now read the topic sentence yet again. If the topic sentence seems adequate to prepare the reader for the material in the rest of the paragraph, remove the asterisks.
3. If the topic sentence needs more work, press the carriage return to separate the sentence from the rest of the paragraph and skip a line. Working beneath the original topic sentence, draft as many new versions as necessary to unify the other sentences and better prepare the reader for the other material in the paragraph. Try to define with more clarity the central idea of the paragraph. When you are satisfied with your revision, delete the other versions and close up the paragraph by removing the empty lines and spaces.
4. If the topic sentence is implied (typed in capital letters), consider making it a permanent part of the sentence. If it will improve the clarity of the paragraph, include it by

* Albert Mehrabian, "Communication Without Words," *Psychology Today* 2, 4 (1968): 53–55.

switching the letters in the sentence from upper to lower case and removing the space that separates it from the rest of the sentence. If it does not improve clarity, delete the implied topic sentence.

Recall that the student in our example identified the first sentence in the paragraph as the topic sentence. As he reads through the rest of the paragraph, he notes that the bulk of the paragraph explains what body movements contribute to nonverbal communication. When he turns to the topic sentence, however, he finds that it does not indicate *why* body movements are important. So, he decides to revise this topic sentence. He first separates the topic sentence from the rest of the paragraph by inserting carriage returns. Then, leaving the original topic sentence intact for reference, he types a revised version.

***** According to Mehrabian, a third type of nonverbal communication is changes in body movements. *****

According to Mehrabian, changes in body movements, a third type of nonverbal communication, indicate both positive and negative attitudes of speakers and listeners.

FIGURE 45. A topic sentence revision.

Revise Other Sentences in the Paragraph to Fit with the New Topic Sentence

Often, when you change the topic sentence, you must revise other sentences to give your paragraph coherence and unity. After you have revised the topic sentence, use the following procedure to check the rest of the sentences in the paragraph.

CHECKING FOR COHERENCE AND UNITY AFTER TOPIC SENTENCE IS REVISED

1. Scroll through the paragraph and delete all sentences that do not support the new topic sentence.
2. Scroll again through the paragraph and add material to provide additional support for the topic sentence.
3. Scroll once more through the paragraph and add transitional expressions and other connecting devices to improve unity and coherence.

Let's return for the last time to the student in our example. After he revised his topic sentence, he reread the paragraph, keeping the new topic sentence in mind. He deleted the second and fourth sentences since he felt that they did not contribute to the main idea of the paragraph. Then he added a sentence that explains how listeners' body movements can convey positive feelings. At this point, the student decided to move the examples of positive attitudes to the first part of the paragraph. Finally, he added transitional elements. Compare the revised paragraph to the original version in Figures 46 and 47.

According to Mehrabian, a third type of nonverbal communication is changes in body movements. Facial expressions, scratching, hand, arm, and leg movements are examples. Speakers who frequently move their heads or limbs unveil a fidgity, uninterested attitude towards their listeners. Changes in people's body movements also indicate how anxious they are in social situations. For example, listeners who constantly shift in their chairs convey to speakers that they are either bored or anxious. As people speak, if they lean toward their listeners, they show they are feeling positive. If listeners nod their heads in agreement, they are showing that they respond positively to the speakers' words.

Figure 46. Original paragraph (see Figure 47 for revision).

> According to Mehrabian, changes in body movements, a third type of nonverbal communication, indicate both positive and negative attitudes of speakers and listeners. As people speak, if they lean toward the listeners, they are showing that they are feeling positive. Similarly, if listeners nod their heads in agreement, they are showing that they respond positively to the speakers' words. On the other hand, speakers who move their heads or limbs frequently, unveil a fidgity, uninterested attitude towards their listeners. Likewise, listeners who constantly shift in their chairs convey to speakers that they are either bored or anxious.

FIGURE 47. Revised paragraph.

Revise Paragraphs That Have No Topic Sentences, Either Stated or Implied

In cases where there is neither an explicit nor an implied topic sentence you will need to restructure the paragraph so that it develops a single idea. Use the following procedure, which combines elements of several techniques described earlier:

REVISING PARAGRAPHS THAT HAVE NO TOPIC SENTENCES
1. Read through the paragraph and then type in at the beginning of the paragraph a topic sentence that expresses what you mean to say. 2. Scroll through the paragraph and delete all sentences that do not support the new topic sentence. 3. Scroll again through the paragraph and add material to provide additional support for the topic sentence. 4. Scroll once more through the paragraph and add transitional expressions and other connecting devices to improve unity and coherence.

Introductions and Conclusions

Review the guidelines for writing introductions and conclusions presented in Chapter 4. Recall that the purpose of the introductory paragraph is to forecast the general topic area and to present the thesis if there is one. Check once again to see that the thesis statement expresses the main idea you want to communicate in the paper. Make sure that the introduction does not promise anything you fail to deliver in the body of the paper. Recall that the conclusion may summarize the high points of the paper, but you should also use closing techniques like (1) stressing the significance of your ideas, (2) predicting the consequences of your ideas, (3) calling your readers to action, and (4) ending with a question, anecdote, or quotation. Note that the introduction and conclusion may follow somewhat different patterns of development from that of the other paragraphs in the paper. For instance, the introductory paragraph often ends with the thesis statement, whereas paragraphs in the body of the essay typically begin with a topic sentence. Figures 48 and 49 are examples of student Maura Kennedy's introduction and conclusion.

> Although we hate to admit it, many governments have failed to heed George Orwell's predictive and quite disturbing warnings in *1984*. Perhaps the most obvious examples are the Communist nations. However, "the Commies" are not the only ones at fault. Many democratic, capitalistic governments sometimes work like the totalitarian government of Orwell's Oceania. Events like those in *1984* have already occurred in Communist China in the recent past. But perhaps even more frightening is that they are happening right now in the United States and could be expanded here in the future.

Figure 48. Maura Kennedy's introduction.

It is frightening to see that events like those in *1984*, a novel written with the intent of carrying a warning, have already happened, are happening, and will happen again in real life. The parallels between China and Oceania, Mao Zedong and Big Brother are disturbingly real. In America the FCC's control of radio now limits "free-speech" and could possibly end up distorting facts and brainwashing the public. Although this happening to the extent as in *1984* is doubtful, it is possible. Our own "Thought Police" FBI with their version of the telescreen may be coming in the near future. *1984* may not have come to the United States in its predicted year, but that doesn't mean that it will never come.

Figure 49. Maura Kennedy's conclusion.

CONNECTIONS BETWEEN IDEAS

After you have reviewed your paragraphs to check for topic sentences, the next step is to check that the sentences in each paragraph cohere or stick together. Viewing each paragraph as a separate unit, ask yourself these questions:

CHECKING FOR COHERENCE

1. Have I structured the paragraph according to a recognizable pattern that reveals the relationships among the ideas?
2. Have I used effective devices to highlight the connections between ideas and thus shown how one sentence relates to another?

When you are considering the paragraph as a separate unit, it helps to see on the page or screen just one paragraph at a time. Using your word processor, you can view entire paragraphs in isolation either on the screen or in a printout. Probably the majority of your paragraphs will fit on a single computer screen. If you want to see the paragraph in complete isolation on the screen, you can insert extra carriage returns before and after the paragraph until only the one paragraph is left. If you are working with printout, fold the paper, regardless of its perforation, so that you see only the one paragraph.

Organizational Patterns

Earlier in this chapter you analyzed your paper as a whole in order to determine the most appropriate organizational plan for it. Now you can do the same type of analysis at the paragraph level. You will recall that in Chapter 3 we presented a list of the ways writers order ideas. Now we will illustrate some patterns of paragraph development. The methods of development you will use most often are description, time order, narration, process analysis, definition, classification, example, comparison and contrast, and cause and effect.

Description: Use description to develop your topic by giving its attributes, parts, or setting. You may want to make an impression on your reader's senses by using details that allow the reader to imagine whatever you are describing, or you may want to give your reader a technical description that includes the exact specifications of the object, person, or scene.

Notice how vividly Thoreau conveys the scene he experiences in "A Winter Walk":

> In this glade covered with bushes of a year's growth, see how the silvery dust lies on every seared leaf and twig, deposited in such infinite and luxurious forms as by their very variety atone for the absence of color. Observe the tiny tracks of mice around every stem, and the triangular tracks of the rabbit. A pure elastic heaven hangs over all, as if the impurities of the summer sky, refined and shrunk by the chaste winter's cold, had been winnowed from the heavens upon the earth.

Time Order: A paragraph developed by time order presents a series of events in chronological order:

> Charles Dicken's attitude toward society and its effect on individuals changes over the course of his career. In his early novels, Dickens is optimistic. He feels that negative social forces are powerless against human innocence and goodness. In the world of *Pickwick Papers* (1836–37) life is basically good. Evil is present, but it is not a threat. Innocence revels in innumerable romantic experiences. Then, in *Oliver Twist* (1837–39), even though innocence is continually threatened and stripped naked by a wicked social system, it persists in

goodness and remains unstained until it is rescued by external forces. Thirteen years later in *Bleak House*, however, Dickens demonstrates that the individual can no longer rely on benevolent individuals for salvation. At this point Dickens insists that in order to remain innocent people must disengage themselves from society and actually deny social will. Continuing in this vein, in *Little Dorrit* (1855–57) Dickens shows that Amy has to privately reject worldliness and recognize where her duty lies before she can save herself. Last, in *Great Expectations* (1860–61) Dickens has Pip succumb to temptation, negate childlike simplicity, and sacrifice himself to his social ambitions. Not until he is forced to choose decisively—to openly revolt against society and give up the attractive life for which he longed—is he able to re-create his former innocence and save himself.

Narration: Another paragraph developed by time order is a narrative paragraph. This type of paragraph usually tells a story. The writer may incorporate flashbacks or flashforwards and may build towards a climax or turning point. The writer may also relay a straightforward sequence of events. Consider the following paragraph from Mark Twain's *Roughing It*. Lost in a snow storm, Twain and his companions attempt to build a campfire:

> We huddled together on our knees in the deep snow, and the horses put their noses together and bowed their patient heads over us; and while the feathering flakes eddied down and turned us into a group of white statuary, we proceeded with the momentous experiment. We broke twigs from a sage brush and piled them on a little cleared place in the shelter of our bodies. In the course of ten or fifteen minutes all was ready, and then, while conversation ceased and our pulses beat low with anxious suspense, Ollendorff applied his revolver, pulled the trigger and blew the pile clear out of the county! It was the flattest failure that ever was.

Process Analysis: Like a narrative paragraph, a paragraph developed by process analysis presents a sequence of events. In a process paragraph, however, the events are causally related; one action leads to another. The following paragraph describes the chain-reaction process:

> The fission reaction is the actual source of energy in a nuclear power plant. The core of the reactor contains rods made of the element uranium 235. The fission of a U-235 atom takes place when a neutron strikes the nucleus of the atom and splits the original atom into several smaller atoms. The smaller atoms taken together contain less matter than the original U-235 atom did. At the moment of fission, some of the matter is converted directly into energy. This energy is used to heat up water to produce steam. The steam in turn drives turbines that produce the electric power the plant provides. The fission reaction gives off neutrons that are not bonded to atoms. These neutrons can collide with and split other U-235 atoms. The process of one fission reaction leading to another is called a "chain reaction." Chain reactions are kept under control by inserting material into the reactor core that absorbs neutrons and thus slows down the rate at which the reaction spreads through the nuclear fuel.

Definition: A paragraph developed by definition offers the reader an explanation of a key term. A clear-cut definition will allow the reader to get a firm grasp of your ideas. You may recall that in Chapter 5 we saw how a writer improved her first draft by adding a definition paragraph after the introduction:

> Genetic engineering involves at least three distinct processes: gene splicing, cloning, and selective breeding. Gene splicing and cloning are new techniques that scientists have successfully performed with lower animals and are contemplating using with humans. Gene splicing involves replacing parts of an organism's genetic structure in order to change its characteristics. For example, a defective gene that causes Down's syndrome could be replaced with a normal gene, thus eliminating the disorder. Cloning is making an exact copy of an organism by extracting some of its genetic material and using it to grow a new individual. Whereas in normal reproduction the offspring's genetic material is a combination of the genes of two parents, the clone obtains all its genes from one parent. The third genetic engineering technique, selective breeding, has been practiced for thousands of years with plants and animals and to some extent with humans. Selective breeding of humans requires that the parents be chosen carefully so that they will provide their offspring with genes for desirable traits.

Classification: In a classification paragraph, you explain the topic by grouping its parts according to their common characteristics:

> The types of physical changes occurring during adolescence are pubertal changes, changes in height and weight, and changes in sexual characteristics. The two most dramatic pubertal changes are the growth spurt and the maturation of sexual organs. Other changes include breast development, growth of pubic hair, and development of sweat glands.

Example: In a paragraph developed by example, you give your reader concrete illustrations or instances of the ideas you want to discuss:

> Linguists have observed that when young children are in the "holophrastic speech stage," the stage when they produce single loud utterances, they understand and intend more than they actually say. For example, "Cookie" may mean "There is the box of cookies," "I want a cookie," or "I dropped my cookie." The single word utterance is assumed to be a sentence.

Comparison and Contrast: A paragraph developed by comparison gives similarities, whereas a paragraph developed by contrast shows differences. There are two major ways to compare and contrast elements: the *block* presentation and the *point-by-point* presentation. Using the block format, you first present all the information about element *A* and then all the information about element *B*. With the point-by-point format, you alternate, presenting one item of information about *A* followed by one item of information about *B*, followed by another item about *A* and another about *B*, and so forth. Compare the two paragraphs that follow, both of which are from Henry Adams's *The Education of Henry Adams.*

BLOCK FORMAT

Winter and summer, cold and heat, town and country, force and freedom, marked two modes of life and thought, balanced like lobes of the brain. Town was winter, confinement, school, rule, discipline; straight, gloomy streets piled with six feet of snow in the middle; frosts that made the snow sing under wheels or runners; thaws when the street became dangerous to cross; society of uncles, aunts, and cousins who expected children to behave themselves, and who were not always gratified; above all else, winter represented the desire to escape and go free. Town was restraint, law, unity. Country, only seven miles away, was liberty, diversity, outlawry, the endless delight of mere sense impressions given by nature for nothing, and breathed by boys without knowing it.

POINT-BY-POINT FORMAT

Winter and summer, then, were two hostile lives, and bred two separate natures. Winter was always the effort to live; summer was tropical license. Whether the children rolled in the grass or waded in the brook, or swam in the salt ocean, or sailed in the bay, or fished for smelts in the creeks, or netted minnows in the salt marshes, or took to the pine-woods and the granite quarries, chased muskrats or hunted snapping-turtles in the swamps, or mushrooms or nuts in the autumn hills, summer and country were always sensual living, while winter was always compulsory learning. Summer was the multiplicity of nature; winter was school.

Cause and Effect: A *cause* precedes or comes before something else. An *effect* comes after, or results from, something else. In a cause-and-effect paragraph, the cause comes before the effect and usually makes the effect happen. As you read the following paragraph, look for the cause and the effect.

Since 1870 over two-thirds of public school teachers in the United States have been female. Yet the history of the schools is shaped and written by men. The reasons why men have dominated the American educational establishment are twofold. First, men hold almost all leadership positions as superintendents, administrators, and supervisors of schools. Second, men also control leadership positions in teachers' associations, research organizations, and professional educational associations.

REVISING PARAGRAPH PATTERNS

Now review each of your paragraphs to see if you have used any of the patterns of development discussed above or any of the other patterns listed on page 53. Then review each of your paragraphs to see if you have ordered your ideas according to one of these plans. To do this effectively, try the following procedures:

CHECKING FOR ORGANIZATIONAL PATTERNS

1. Move the cursor to the top of the file, and skip over the introduction to the next paragraph.
2. Read through the paragraph and identify the organizational plan that ties together the sentences in the paragraph. In capital letters, type in the name of this pattern on the line directly above the paragraph. If you cannot see a pattern, type a question mark. Go through the same procedure for all paragraphs except for the introduction and the conclusion.
3. Return to the top of the file, and skip over the introduction to the next paragraph. Note the organizational plan and read through the paragraph looking for any sentences that do not fit with this plan and for any sequence of sentences that does not fit it. Make any changes that are needed to support the plan.
4. If the paragraph has no clear organizational plan, read the topic sentence, look through the paragraph patterns discussed on page 104, and think of one or more patterns that could develop the idea expressed in the topic sentence. Revise the paragraph, retaining only those sentences from the original that fit the new pattern; if necessary, add new sentences to develop the pattern.
5. Apply this procedure to all paragraphs except for the introduction and conclusion. When you are finished, make sure that you delete all the capitalized plan names.

Here is how one student used this procedure on a rough-draft paragraph.

PLAN: CAUSE—EFFECT OR COMPARE—CONTRAST?

Sex-typing children stifles their creativity. If a child is expected to adhere to a specific sex role, he or she will have limitations. Within the past ten years there has been a great deal done to promote sexual equality. When I think back to my early school years, I remember how I always played in the doll corner with my girlfriends. Last summer, when I worked at a nursery school, however, the boys played house and the girls played with cars and trucks. Today, children have fewer sexual limitations than they did in the past; therefore, they are more creative on a social and academic level. If teachers put less emphasis on traditional sex roles, children would have the opportunity for more experiences.

FIGURE 50. Paragraph pattern rough draft.

PLAN: COMPARE—CONTRAST

Within the past ten years schools have put less emphasis on sex-typing children, and teachers have done much to promote sexual equality. When I think back to my early school years, I remember how I always played in the doll corner with my girlfriends. When I lost interest in playing house, the teacher encouraged me to read books. Last summer when I worked in a nursery school, however, the teacher set up situations in which the boys and girls played house together. In addition, she encouraged the girls to work on block-building projects and to play with cars and trucks. Today, because teachers put less emphasis on traditional sex roles, children have fewer limitations in sex roles than they did in the past.

FIGURE 51. Paragraph pattern revision.

When the student read through the rough draft, she had difficulty deciding whether the ideas were arranged according to a cause-effect plan or a comparison-contrast plan. The first two sentences suggest that the paragraph will show how sex-typing limits children's creativity, but the bulk of the paragraph compares sex-typing ten years ago with sex-typing today. The writer saw that there is very little cause or effect in this development, and so she opted for the plan of compare and contrast. She deleted sentences one and two and let the third sentence stand as the topic sentence. Then she revised the paragraph by retaining the ideas that fit the comparison pattern and adding a sentence and transitions that would further develop this plan.

Cohesion

After you have checked that you have ordered your paragraphs according to an adequate organizational plan, examine them more closely to see if they are *cohesive*. Cohesive paragraphs have sentences whose ideas connect with each other. "Links" or "ties" within these paragraphs act to unite the sentences. They help readers to follow the train of thought by referring back to the preceding sentence(s) or ahead to the sentence(s) that follow.

Some common connective devices are the following:*

CONNECTIVE DEVICES
• Repeating words or parts of words • Substituting synonyms, near-synonyms, or related words • Using personal pronouns and demonstrative pronouns (*this, that*) with easily recognizable referents • Using explicit or implied transitions that signal relations like addition, exemplification, opposition, similarity, cause, effect, or time order • Substituting a general term for a more specific term or terms

Figure 52 shows a paragraph in which a student has used a number of connective devices. We have highlighted and labeled some of them; see if you can find others.

FIGURE 52. Connective devices.†

A Separate Peace shows that SARCASM
helps us to escape from stating the truth
straightforwardly. Gene, the weaker
Repeats Word
character, uses SARCASM to express DISAP-

* Adapted from M. A. K. Halliday and Ruquaiya Hasan, *Cohesion in English* (London: Longman), 1976.

† Knowles, John. *A Separate Peace*. New York: Macmillan, 1969.

Transition: Contrast	PROVAL, WHEREAS Finny, the symbol of	Synonym
Repeats Word	strength, blatantly STATES his DISAPPROVAL.	Transition: Cause
	Gene uses SARCASM BECAUSE he feels	
Pronoun	resentment towards Finny. HIS INDIGNATION	Synonym
Demonstrative Pronoun	stems from JEALOUSY. THIS becomes evident	
	after Finny charms his way out of trouble for	
	wearing the Devon tie as a belt. Gene	
	explains, "He had gotten away with every-	
	thing. I felt a sudden stab of disappoint-	
Transition: Time	ment." LATER, HE adds, "That was because I	Pronoun
	just wanted to see some more excitement;	
	that must have been it" (Knowles 21).	
Transition: Contrast	ALTHOUGH Gene's JEALOUSY almost causes	Repeats Word
	him to dislike Finny, he cannot admit this	
General Term	PAINFUL FACT, and he covers IT up.	Pronoun

Try a similar procedure on selected paragraphs from your own rough drafts to get a rough idea of how effectively you use transitional expressions.

CHECKING TRANSITIONAL EXPRESSIONS

1. Either at the beginning of your draft file or in a separate textfile, use the cut-and-paste function to make *duplicates* of the paragraphs you intend to analyze. Do not delete the paragraphs from the original draft; merely duplicate them.

2. Read carefully the list of connective devices given above. (If your word processor allows you to split the screen or open windows, you can type the list into a textfile and display it on the screen along with the rough draft you are checking.)
3. Scroll through your rough draft and capitalize all the letters in any of the connective devices you notice. (Many word processors allow you to capitalize entire words that were originally typed in lower case by using a single command.)
4. Print out the paragraphs you analyzed. Read each paragraph and see if your transitional expressions support the paragraph's overall organizational pattern. If necessary, add or alter transitional expressions in the original draft.

Since this procedure is time consuming, you probably will not use it on every rough draft, but you may wish to use it occasionally to check your use of transitions.

Try to identify the connective devices from Figure 52 that the student used in two other paragraphs in her paper (Figure 53).

I have often tried to cover up the truth as well. I once had a very close friend, "Sally," whom I gradually came to despise. I kept telling myself that Sally was conceited and cared about no one but herself. I later realized that I, being shy, was jealous of her outgoing personality and her ability to make people like her. And just as Gene realizes that he and Finny aren't "competitors," that Finny has always thought of him as his best friend and would never do anything to hurt him, so I realized the same about my friend. Then I became even more annoyed, because even though I was rude to Sally, she still thought of me as her best friend. My annoyance caused a resentment that eventually ended our friendship. By the time I realized this, we were both better friends with other people. Gene also realizes too late that his competition with Finny "was so ludicrous [he] wanted to cry" (Knowles 58). I too found this out after Sally and I had stopped being best friends. And like Gene, I still think about it today, three years later.

FIGURE 53. Connective devices employed (see Figure 52).

Gene meanwhile fools himself by making up stories. So does Finny. When Gene gets Leper's telegram, he immediately imagines Leper escaping from spies. He lets himself believe this because deep down he knows that whatever has happened to Leper probably isn't as exciting as his imaginative prediction. When Leper's real reason for "escaping" shatters his hopes, Gene must deal with the unpleasant truth that he had been avoiding. Although Finny's character is in many ways stronger than Gene's, Finny also makes up his own stories about the war in order to escape from reality. Finny doesn't want to accept the fact that he won't be fighting in the war. Because he doesn't like this idea, he tries to convince himself and others that there is really no war at all. To him "the fat old men" in the government have made up the war (Knowles 107). He finally faces the truth about the war when he sees Leper. Knowles shows that even strong people like Finny delude themselves from recognizing an unpleasant truth.

FIGURE 53. (continued)

EXERCISE 6

Choose three paragraphs from one of your rough drafts. Analyze and revise each paragraph as follows:

1. Check and, if necessary, revise the topic sentence using the procedure described on page 96.
2. Check and, if necessary, revise the organizational pattern using the procedure described on page 108.
3. Check and, if necessary, revise the connective devices using the procedure described on page 111.

SEVEN
REVISING STYLE

Our discussion of style in this brief chapter only scratches the surface of a very complex topic. We have to stress that stylistic revision on the word processor cannot be as rule-driven and systematic as electronic proofreading, which we discuss in Chapter 8. Indeed, good style depends heavily on the context of the piece of writing. A major weakness of commercially available "style-checker" programs is that they reduce style to a set of simple, programmable rules. Whatever good style may be, it is unlikely that it will result from the mindless application of computerized procedures.

We will discuss using the word processor not only to correct problems in your style but also to develop an awareness of your stylistic choices. The first step in gaining control of your writing style is to understand how you habitually use written language. Then you need to consider the effect your choices have on an audience. For example, many students habitually write sentences that are the same length without ever considering that an audience might find this style boring and monotonous. The word processor can help you manipulate the text of a paper so that you can display the lengths of your sentences graphically. Once you have analyzed your style, you can use the word processor to make stylistic changes.

IDENTIFYING AND MODIFYING YOUR PERSONAL PROSE SYTLE

Sentence Length and Shape

Readers often become bored and confused when they face numerous sentences in a row of the same length and structure. Note the monotony in the following example:

> Another problem with Farber's argument is the lack of sufficient evidence. Farber uses strictly personal experiences to show that grades don't work. He could have used examples from other people or from other books. Also, he might have cited statistics from research studies and experiments.

Writers interested in improving their style should vary sentence length and syntax. Without the benefit of computer technology, you would have to count and record the number of words in each sentence to determine whether or not you are varying that number as your write. With your word processor, however, you can determine length by printing out a version of the paper in which each sentence appears in isolation. In order to do this, use either of the following procedures.

ISOLATING SENTENCES
• Scroll through the paper and insert two carriage returns after each sentence. Then, print out a single-spaced version of the paper. OR • If you have a search-and-replace feature, use it to locate each period. Replace each with a period and two carriage returns. Do the same for question marks and exclamation points. Then, print out a single-spaced version of the paper.

After you have printed out the sentence individually, you can see at a glance, without counting individual words, whether you vary sentence length or not. If you leave all pages of the printout attached and look sideways, you have a rough bar graph of sentence length. Consider the passage we discussed earlier (Figure 54). In contrast, look at a passage containing sentences of varied lengths. The excerpt appears first as a paragraph (Figure 55) and then in bar graph form (Figure 56).

FIGURE 54. Isolated sentences of uniform length.

Another problem with Farber's argument is the lack of sufficient evidence.

Farber uses strictly personal experiences to show that grades don't work.

He could have used examples from other people or from other books.

Also, he might have cited statistics from research studies and experiments.

The primary issue here is safety. Statistics reveal that seat belts save the lives of people riding in cars. But what effect do they have on passengers in school buses? According to a recent Pennsylvania study, 75 percent of accidents involving children and school buses happened outside the vehicles, as students crossed the street and were injured by careless motorists. Of the accidents occurring on the bus, only 3.6 percent were of a serious nature. Moreover, if these children had been belted, the injuries would not have been prevented (Dickson).

FIGURE 55. Excerpt from student Betsy Fowlson's paper.*

* Herbert Dickson, principal of Greene Central School, Greene, N.Y. Personal interview, April 13, 1987.

The primary issue here is safety.

But what effect do they have on passengers in school buses?

Statistics reveal that seat belts save the lives of people riding in cars.

Of the accidents occurring on the bus, only 3.6 percent were of a serious nature.

Moreover, if these children had been belted, the injuries would not have been prevented (Dickson).

According to a recent Pennsylvania study, 75 percent of accidents involving children and school buses happened outside the vehicles, as students crossed the street and were injured by careless motorists.

Figure 56. Isolated sentences of varied length.

Notice that the student has used short sentences for basic statements, questions, and generalizations and long sentences for examples and supporting details. Writers often use short sentences to highlight their most important ideas. In any case, strive for a mix of lengths to keep your prose varied and interesting.

Combining and Dividing Sentences

When you discover a problem with sentence length, a workable solution is combining or dividing sentences. Your word processor will facilitate both of these operations. First, we will look at sentence combining. Consider the following paragraph, where all sentences are relatively short:

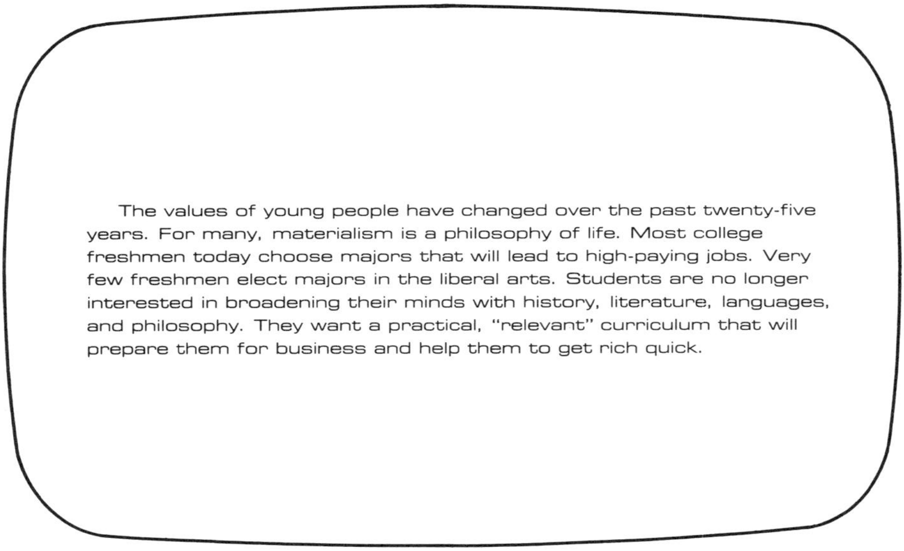

The values of young people have changed over the past twenty-five years. For many, materialism is a philosophy of life. Most college freshmen today choose majors that will lead to high-paying jobs. Very few freshmen elect majors in the liberal arts. Students are no longer interested in broadening their minds with history, literature, languages, and philosophy. They want a practical, "relevant" curriculum that will prepare them for business and help them to get rich quick.

FIGURE 57. Example of a paragraph with short sentences.

To combine sentences, start at the beginning of the paragraph and move the cursor to the boundary of the first sentence. Many word processors have a single command that will move the cursor from any point in a sentence to the end of the sentence. At each boundary, consider whether or not it makes sense to combine the two sentences. Working with the above example, you might stop at sentence 3 and sentence 4. You could combine these sentences using any of the following techniques:

COMBINING SENTENCES

1. Join independent clauses with coordinating conjunctions (*and, but for, or, nor, yet, so*):
   Most college freshmen today choose majors that will lead to high-paying jobs, so very few elect majors in the liberal arts.
2. Join independent clauses with adverbial conjunctions (*however, consequently, thus, furthermore, nevertheless, then, certainly, besides, similarly,* and so on):
   Most college freshman today choose majors that will lead to high-paying jobs; consequently, very few freshmen elect majors in the liberal arts.
3. Embed one sentence within another sentence:
   The trend for most college freshman today to choose majors leading to high-paying jobs means that very few elect majors in the liberal arts.
4. Change an independent clause to a dependent clause and use a subordinator (*since, if, because, unless,* and so on) to relate it to an independent clause.
   Because most college freshman today choose majors that will lead to high-paying jobs, very few elect majors in the liberal arts.

Make sure that all sentence combinations contribute to clarity and coherence. Remember not to combine at every sentence boundary, since your goal is variety not consistency.

To divide a long sentence, scroll through the sentence looking for clause boundaries. Clauses are basic idea units structured with a subject and a verb. Try to subdivide the sentence at these clause boundaries. The following procedures will help you locate clause boundaries and divide sentences.

DIVIDING LONG SENTENCES ON THE WORD PROCESSOR

1. Search for coordinating conjunctions (*and, but, for, or, nor, yet, so*) and for adverbial conjunctions (*however,*

nevertheless, consequently, thus, and so on) and try to divide sentences at these points.

2. Search for subordinating conjunctions (*if, when, unless, because, although,* and so on) and try to break up the sentence by turning the dependent clause into an independent clause.
3. Look for other incidents of *and* or *but* between multiple verbs sharing a subject and try to divide the sentence by inserting a period before the conjunction and inventing a subject for the second verb.

Consider how Carrie Miller, a student writer, used these procedures to revise a paragraph from her research paper on acid rain.

Acid rain has been with us for longer than most people realize, for the term "acid rain" was originally coined back in 1872 when British chemist Robert Angus Smith noticed that buildings were being worn away by rain falling on industrial England (Begley 9). Acid rain is caused by sulfur emissions from burning soft coal and other fossil fuels. These particles become airborne and eventually settle back to earth via precipitation, which changes the pH of the water and soil; consequently, as Smith observed, the acid pits and crumbles buildings. We know what the acid rain does to lakes and forests is even more harmful because Anne LaBastille, wildlife ecologist and consultant, points out that in the Adirondack area where she lives, "Thirty-five percent of the big trees were dead or dying" (96). Another observer complains that the Adirondack region has about 520 lakes that are suffering from rain pollution (LaFave 42). Acid rain leaves a lake crystal clear and void of many species of fish. An analogy would be a bottle of vinegar, which has a pH of 5, and much of the rainfall in the eastern United States measures 4.5 on the pH scale, which means that rainfall is *more* acid than vinegar. Certainly, the rain is diluted as it soaks into the ground, but the effects are cumulative (Krester 25).

FIGURE 58. Carrie Miller's first draft.*

After scrolling through the paragraph, the student decided to break up the first, third, fourth, and seventh sentences. Compare the revised version to the original.

* Sharon Begley, "On the Trail of Acid Rain," *National Wildlife* (February–March 1987): 8–13; Walter A. Krester, James R. Colquhoun, and Martin H. Pfeiffer, "Acid Rain and the Adirondack Sport Fishery," *The Conservationist* (March–April 1983): 22–29; Anne LaBastille, *Beyond Black Bear Lake*, New York: Norton, 1987; Aziel LaFave, "Reflections of Terror Lake," *The Conservationist* (July–August 1983): 38–42.

Acid rain has been with us for longer than most people realize. The term "acid rain" was originally coined back in 1872 when British chemist Robert Angus Smith noticed that buildings were being worn away by rain falling on industrial England (Begley 9). Acid rain is caused by sulfur emissions from burning soft coal and other fossil fuels. These particles become airborne and eventually settle back to earth via precipitation, which changes the pH of the water and soil. Consequently, as Smith observed, the acid pits and crumbles buildings. We know what the acid rain does to lakes and forests is even more harmful. Anne LaBastille, wildlife ecologist and consultant, points out that in the Adirondack area where she lives, "Thirty-five percent of the big trees were dead or dying" (96). Another observer complains that the Adirondack region has about 520 lakes that are suffering from rain pollution (LaFave 42). Acid rain leaves a lake crystal clear and void of many species of fish. An analogy would be a bottle of vinegar, which has a pH of 5. Much of the rainfall in the eastern United States measures 4.5 on the pH scale, which means that rainfall is *more* acid than vinegar. Certainly, the rain is diluted as it soaks into the ground, but the effects are cumulative (Krester 25).

FIGURE 59. Carrie Miller's revision.

Stressing Verbs Rather Than Nouns

Good writers express action with specific or strong verbs. They shy away from empty verbs and they avoid using too many nouns. Compare the following sentences. In the first version the writer uses nouns to get the message across, but in the revised version he relies upon verbs. We have underlined the nouns and italicized the verbs.

Original: The creation of an overall design for a computer system *is* the responsibility of a systems analyst, whereas the implementation of the design plan *is* often the duty of a computer programmer.

Revision: The system analyst *designs* the computer system, and the computer programmer *makes* the system *work.*

Notice that the first version contains two occurrences of the verb *is. Is* and other forms of the verb *be* (*are, was, were, be, being, been*) draw their meaning from the nouns that precede and follow them; they are weak and lifeless on their own. Thus, sentences structured around *be* verbs depend on the nouns to convey the central ideas. These "noun-style" sentences are characterized by forms of the verb *be* (*is, are,* and so on) and by nominalization, the practice of making nouns from verbs or adjectives by adding suffixes (*-ance, -ence, -tion, -ment, -sion*). The nouns in these sentences often appear in prepositional phrases; an additional sign of nominalization is frequent use of prepositions. Below, we have underlined the *be* verb forms, the instances of nominalization, and the prepositions in the sentence we considered earlier. Notice that the revision does not rely on *be* verbs or nominalization.

> **Original:** The creation of an overall design for a computer system is the responsibility of a systems analyst, whereas the implementation of the design plan is often the duty of a computer programmer.
>
> **Revision:** The systems analyst designs the computer system, and the computer programmer makes the system work.

You can determine the extent to which you overuse *be* verbs by highlighting these forms with the search- and -replace function of your word processor. Locate the cursor at the beginning of the paper and set the search-and-replace function to locate "is" and replace it with "IS" throughout the document. Repeat this procedure for the other common *be* verbs forms: *are, was, were,* and *be.* Follow a similar procedure to locate the cases of nominalization. This time, use the word processor search-and-replace function to capitalize each of the noun suffixes ("ance," "ence," "tion," "ment", "sion"). For example, a search for "tion" would locate the two cases of nominalization in the example above. Since nominalization often involves overuse of prepositions, you might also use the search and replace function to highlight the most common prepositions ("of," "on," "to," "in," and so on). When you print out your paper, the *be* verbs, prepositions, and nominalizations will stand out as they do in the following example:

FIGURE 60. Highlighting "be" verbs, prepositions, and nominalizations.

ARE sexual differences biologically based or ARE they caused BY the environment? This controversial issue IS one which has gained much attention IN the past decade and IS still the cause OF argumentaTION today. Granted, one may argue ON the basis OF studies done ON primates that the inferiority women face today IS biologically based. One might also claim that the physical differences IN males and females ARE justificaTION FOR giving men and women different roles and that distinct differences IN the brains OF men and women ARE verficaTION that their thinking skills contrast greatly. These claimes ARE valid TO a certain extent; however, other noted professionals ARE in disagreeMENT. They claim that the discrepancy IN male and female roles IS the consequENCE OF socially ascribed and accepted "rules" OF society.

SEARCH-AND-REPLACE FILES

Some sophisticated word processors and spelling checkers allow you to establish a file that contains a list of word-for-word replacements that you want to make in other files. Using these capabilities you could establish a file that contains the list of replacements for *be* verbs ("IS" for "is", "WAS" for "was," etc.). With this list you can make changes in other files that contain drafts of papers. Once you have created a search- and -replace file, you can use it to analyze and change as many files as you want. A single command analyzes and changes each new file. You could streamline the process of highlighting *be* verbs, prepositions, and nominalizations by creating a single search- and -replace file for capitalizing all these elements.

WORD FREQUENCY COUNTERS

The word-frequency-count feature on some sophisticated spelling checkers will count all *be* verbs in a paper. Word frequency counters analyze a paper and then list each different word used. Consider the following example from the beginning of a word frequency list:

the	56
a	47
in	23
is	21

To get your *be* verb count, run the word frequency program and either display on the screen or print out the word frequency list. Locate each *be* form and add up the total number of occurrences. Although this procedure gives you a *be* verb count much faster than the search-and-replace method and shows you how often you use *be* verbs in general, you will still have to locate each instance of *be* verbs in context if you want to restructure sentences with more active verbs.

Be aware that even in examples of strong style, you will find *be* verbs and cases of nominalization. Problems in style arise only when these forms are overused. Although there is no absolute rule, you should look closely when you find more than one *be* verb or one nominalization per sentence. You need not analyze the nouns and verbs in every paper you write, but it is a good idea to check periodically the direction in which your style is developing. Over time, you will find that less analysis is necessary since you will tend to use more active verbs and fewer preposition and nominalization structures.

If you decide to minimize the *be* verbs or nominalization in a particular sentence, separate that sentence from context and make a duplicate copy directly below it as we describe on page 98. Then change the duplicate sentence from noun style to verb style.

The announcement of the candidacy of the senator for the office of president was a surprise to the press.

The senator surprised the press when she declared that she would enter the presidential race.

Figure 61. A sentence changed from noun style to verb style.

Using Words Effectively

Clear writing is concise and explicit. It avoids ineffective expressions and words that do not contribute directly to the meaning of the paper. Study the italicized words and phrases in the following passage:

> *Basically*, those in support of surrogate motherhood claim that this *particular* method of reproduction has brought happiness to countless infertile couples. It allows a man to have a child of his own *despite the fact that* his wife cannot bear children. In addition, it is *definitely* preferable to waiting for months and

> sometimes years on *really* long adoption lists. *In my opinion*, however, surrogate motherhood exploits the woman and can be *especially* damaging to the child. *Obviously*, poor women are affected most. *In the event that* a poor couple cannot have a child, it is *rather* unlikely that they will be able to afford the services of a surrogate mother. *Actually*, it is fertile, poor women who become "breeders" for the infertile rich. In any case, the child is *especially* vulnerable. The *given* baby may become involved in a custody battle betweeen the surrogate mother and the adopting mother. If the *individual* child is born handicapped, he or she may be *utterly* rejected by both mothers. *Surely*, the child's welfare should be *first and foremost* in everyone's mind.

Notice that none of these highlighted elements furthers the writer's intentions. They are inherently vague, overused, hackneyed words and phrases or unnecessary qualifiers, intensifiers, or modifiers. Below is a list of some ineffective expressions that occur frequently in student writing:

INEFFECTIVE WORDS AND PHRASES		
a bit	given (used as adjective)	quite
absolutely	individual (used as adjective)	rather
actually	kind of	really
awesome	little	simply
basically	merely	somewhat
certain	most	sort of
certainly	obviously	specific
definitely	particularly	surely
especially	practically	unique
generally	pretty	utterly
		very
in the event that		
in my personal opinion		
the fact that		

With the word processor you can determine how often these words appear in your writing. Use the search function to locate the occurrences and keep a running count. You might limit this search to words from the list that you know you abuse. Then either delete the unnecessary words or replace them with less wordy expressions.

USING WORD FREQUENCY COUNTERS

The word frequency counter, which we described on page 123, can also help you analyze the ways you put your language to work. Produce a word frequency list for your paper and study carefully the words that appear more than three or four times. Does this list suggest that you are repetitious? Do ineffective expressions appear frequently? Do you rely too much on jargon, words that are part of an overspecialized vocabulary? Do you use too much slang?

Writing in First and Second Person

First-person pronouns (*I, my, mine, we, our, ours*) and second-person pronouns (*you, your, yours*) can be appropriate even in formal writing situations. For instance, you will notice that in this textbook we frequently address the audience with the second-person pronouns *you* and *your*. Some students, however, use the first- or second-person in writing where it is not appropriate. Consider the following example from a student's research paper:

Figure 62. Second-person pronouns.

Eighty years ago, when Huey (1908)* wrote about learning to read at home, he noted that the "secret of it all lies in parents' reading aloud to and with the child" (332). Huey's homespun wisdom needs empirical verification. Nonetheless, his basic point remains valid. Numerous studies reveal that either the modeling, the assistance, or simply the presence of an adult is of paramount importance for learning to read. YOU do not set the stage for reading by filling the home with elaborate props. Nor do YOU teach the child his or her lines. Early readers are self-directed learners; they rely on adults only for occasional promptings or clues.

* Edmund B. Huey, *The Psychology and Pedagogy of Reading* (Cambridge, Mass.: MIT Press, 1968 [1908]).

If the writer is addressing parents, the shift to *you* might be appropriate. Since, however, the paragraph is from a research paper, the presence of *you* jars the readers because it implies direction or advice. To keep the passage objective, writer might replace *you* with *parents* or *adults*.

The search- and -replace function can be used to highlight first- and second-person pronouns (see the instructions for highlighting *be* verbs on page 122). Print out your paper, locate these pronouns, and check to see if they are appropriate for the context in which they appear.

Detecting Sexist Language

Good writers avoid sexist language. For example, they use the masculine pronouns *he* and *his* and nouns with "-man" and "-men" (mailman, policemen, and so on) only when they refer to a male or a group composed entirely of males. They do not use these forms to refer to women. Instead, they use pronouns that recognize both sexes ("his or her" or "her or his"), plural pronouns that by their very nature do not specify gender (*they* and *their*), and nouns that are not gender-specific (*mail carrier* and *police officer*). Consider the following example:

> We are increasingly becoming a self-centered society. This obsession with self explains some of the lawlessness on the nation's highways. As each MAN struggles to defend HIS own turf, HE forgets about sharing the road with HIS FELLOW drivers. Impatient, inconsiderate motorists yell, threaten, and physically attack people in nearby cars. They are even more rude to pedestrians. The average MAN on the street puts HIS life in danger every time HE crosses an intersection.

Figure 63. Original draft with sexist language.

> We are increasingly becoming a self-centered society. This obsession with self explains some of the lawlessness on the nation's highways. As motorists struggle to defend their own turf, they forget about sharing the road with other drivers. Impatient, inconsiderate motorists yell, threaten, and physically attack people in nearby cars. They are even more rude to pedestrians. The average person on the street puts his or her life in danger when crossing an intersection.

FIGURE 64. Revision of sexist language.

You can locate instances of sexist language by setting the search- and -replace function to highlight occurrences of *he, his, man* and *men.* Revise to eliminate these forms.

ANALYZING EXPERT WRITING

You can learn about writing style by applying the techniques of analysis that we described in this chapter to the prose of expert writers. Type passages from several nonfiction writers you admire or whom your instructor recommends. Analyze each passage for sentence length, noun and verb style, and so on. What stylistic characteristics do the authors share? What stylistic differences can you detect? Can you account for these differences?

COMPUTERIZED STYLE ANALYSIS

At the beginning of this chapter we cautioned that computerized analysis of style has its limits. Word processors can help you establish more control over your style, but they cannot ultimately solve your stylistic problems. For example, in this chapter we barely mentioned varying style according to context. This is a problem beyond the computer's control. You may find computer programs that are handy for analyzing your style, but you will have to advance beyond their constraints if you want to develop into a sophisticated writer.

EXERCISE 7

Load into the word processor a rough draft of a recent paper. Use the procedures explained in this chapter to analyze and revise your writing style. Perform the following operations:

1. Check that you have varied the length of your sentence by looking at each sentence in isolation. If necessary, combine or divide your sentences.
2. Check that you have expressed action with specific, strong verbs. Use the search-and-replace function to highlight *be* verbs, nominalization, and prepositions. Revise elements that are overused.
3. Review the list of ineffective words and phrases on page 125. Use the word frequency counter to determine how often these words appear in your writing. Then, delete or replace unnecessary words.
4. Set the search-and-replace function to highlight first- and second-person pronouns. Change them if they are inappropriate.
5. Set the search-and-replace function to locate instances of *he, his, man, men,* and revise sexist language.

EIGHT
EDITING GRAMMAR, USAGE, SPELLING, AND MECHANICS

Many student writers dream of a word processor that will rid their rough drafts of grammatical errors, usage problems, and misspellings. No such machine exists, and it is doubtful that it ever will. Word processors cannot automatically correct your grammar any more than they can automatically produce an outline from your rough notes. The responsibility rests with you, not with the computer. Nonetheless, for writers who know the standards of correctness, word processors make it easier to edit effectively.

In this chapter we will explain how you can develop *individualized* techniques for locating and correcting the errors that trip you up most frequently. We recommend that you apply regularly only the techniques that pertain to your own problems. For example, if you know that your writing often contains sentence fragments, you will want to master the procedures we describe in the section on fragments; however, you might ignore the section on subject–verb agreement if you rarely commit errors of this type. Try to identify the subset of electronic proofreading techniques that will serve you best.

Try to customize according to your own needs the proofreading techniques described in this chapter. We do not provide a lock-step set of editing procedures but rather a series of editing possibilities that each reader can adapt. Your word processor can be a versatile editing tool when you use it creatively.

As you work through this chapter, refer to a good writing handbook if you find you lack knowledge of the conventions of correct writing. We will show you how to use word processors to spot and correct some common errors, and we will explain and illustrate them briefly. Nevertheless, this book is not a substitute for a detailed handbook. Furthermore, if you have never examined your writing in order to identify your problem areas, you may need some assistance from your teachers, tutors at your campus writing center, or knowledgeable friends.

SEPARATING SENTENCES FROM CONTEXT

Many writers compose at the word processor, print out their work, and then edit the printed copy. Later, they transfer these changes to the word processor. These writers find it easier to spot problems on the printed page than on a computer screen. There is a distinct advantage to finding errors and editing them on the screen, however, especially if the editing involves making several changes to the same sentence. The machine allows you to isolate a problematic sentence and then produce a second copy for editing while leaving the original sentence intact. Then you can compare your new version to the original, and if the new version is preferable, delete the original. In Figure 65, locate the sentence that needs the most editing.

> Supporters of the nightmarish idea of genetically engineering a superhuman race are misguided individuals. To read about this concept in science fiction is scary enough, but to hear respected scientists seriously promote the idea is even more shocking. To attempt to prevent suffering in the world by using new medicines and related technologies are certainly reasonable, but you can't try to go beyond this and create a race of so-called perfect individuals is absolutely ridiculous and unethical. With such "creatures" in our society, self-determination and individuality would disappear.

FIGURE 65. Sentences and context: excerpt from rough draft.

The third sentence in this excerpt clearly needs editing. The student uses the following procedures:

EDITING SENTENCES

1. Isolate the problematic sentence by inserting carriage returns.
2. Use the cut-and-paste function to make a duplicate of the sentence.
3. Edit the duplicate while leaving the original as is. Produce additional versions of the sentence if necessary.
4. Select the best version and delete the other version(s). Remove the extra lines and spaces to close up the paragraph.

The student first applies Steps 1 and 2:

Supporters of the nightmarish idea of genetically engineering a superhuman race are misguided individuals. To read about this concept in science fiction is scary enough, but to hear respected scientists seriously promote the idea is even more shocking.

To attempt to prevent suffering in the world by using new medicines and related technologies is certainly reasonable, but you can't try to go beyond this and create a race of so-called perfect individuals is absolutely ridiculous and unethical.

To attempt to prevent suffering in the world by using new medicines and related technologies is certainly reasonable, but you can't try to go beyond this and create a race of so-called perfect individuals is absolutely ridiculous and unethical.

With such "creatures" in our society, self-determination and individuality would disappear.

FIGURE 66. Isolating a problematic sentence.

Now, the student can consider the sentence in isolation and work to improve it. By preserving the original, she can better see how she is changing her sentence, and she can continually compare the new version to the original.

Supporters of the nightmarish idea of genetically engineering a superhuman race are misguided individuals. To read about this concept in science fiction is scary enough, but to hear respected scientists seriously promote the idea is even more shocking.

To attempt to prevent suffering in the world by using new medicines and related technologies is certainly reasonable, but to try to go beyond this and create a race of so-called perfect individuals is absolutely ridiculous and unethical.

Scientists should continue to develop new medical technologies aimed at preventing suffering, but attempts to genetically engineer a race of perfect individuals are ridiculous and unethical.

With such "creatures" in our society, self-determination and individuality would disappear.

Figure 67. Editing of a problematic sentence.

In this example the new version of the third sentence is surely preferable to the original. The new version does not contain the grammatical errors and the spelling error that appeared in the original, and it is much easier to understand. If the student feels the sentence needs more work, however, she can produce a third version. In this case the student deletes the original and removes the extra spaces to close up the paragraph (Step 4).

You may find it useful to isolate and examine all the sentences in your paper rather than just the problematic ones. As we will explain later, isolating all your sentences gives you a powerful technique for locating sentence fragments. Use either of the following procedures to look at all your sentences in isolation.

ISOLATING ALL THE SENTENCES IN YOUR PAPER

- Scroll through the paper and insert two carriage returns after each sentence.

OR

- If you have a search-and-replace feature, use it to locate each period. Replace each with a period and two carriage returns. Do the same for question marks and exclamation points.

After you have produced a draft of your paper that lists the sentences separately, print it out. Make sure that you do not destroy the original draft of your paper at any stage of your work on the sentence list.

SENTENCE BOUNDARIES: FRAGMENTS, COMMA SPLICES, AND FUSED SENTENCES

Being able to identify where sentences should begin and end sounds simple, but some problems with sentence boundaries are difficult to recognize. When the problem sentences are surrounded by other sentences in a rough draft, the context tends to hide the difficulties. Consider the following example from a student paper.

> The threat of infection and the possibility of dictators getting control of this powerful new technology are the major risks of genetic engineering. This technology is deceiving, it can have both harmful and helpful results. Commercial exploitation may occur if we are not careful enough. Some scientists and companies are excited about potential profits thus they may not consider the side effects. If by some chance there is an error, worldwide infection may result. Poorer countries will be worse off than more technologically advanced countries. Because they cannot control infection as well.

FIGURE 68. Sentence boundaries: excerpt from a rough draft.

As you read through this sample, you may have noticed that the second sentence has two complete thoughts that are improperly joined by a comma (a comma splice), the fourth sentence has two complete thoughts with no punctuation at all between them (a fused sentence), and the last sentence does not express a complete thought (a fragment). Nevertheless, the paragraph as a whole makes sense when read aloud. The comma splice, fused sentence, and fragment appear as errors only in printed or written form. Thus, to locate comma splices, fused sentences, and fragments it helps to see each sentence in typographical isolation, out of the meaningful context in which it appears.

To locate fragments, comma splices, and fused sentences in your paper, use one of the procedures we outlined above to print out a draft of the paper in which each sentence is isolated from the others. Next, read the list aloud *in reverse order*, that is, starting from the bottom of the list. For an example, look at the following list of sentences from the paragraph we considered earlier. We have positioned them in reverse order so that you can see what it would be like to read them that way.

> Because they cannot control infection as well.
>
> Poorer countries will be worse off than more technologically advanced countries.
>
> If by some chance there is an error, worldwide infection may result.
>
> Some scientists and companies are excited about potential profits, thus they may not consider the side effects
>
> Commercial exploitation may occur if we are not careful enough.
>
> This technology is deceiving, it can have both harmful and helpful results.
>
> The threat of infection and the possibility of dictators getting control of this powerful new technology are the major risks of genetic engineering.

Notice how much easier it is to evaluate the sentences when they are detached from one another rather than grouped together in a paragraph. The fragment leaps to attention when we see it out of context. Reading the sentences in reverse order therefore helps us focus on the individual sentences by disrupting the logical progression of thought in the paragraph.

Once you have located fragments, comma splices, and fused sentences, word processors make it easy to correct them. Since a fragment cannot stand alone, you can combine the fragment with another sentence. In our sample paragraph we can correct the fragment by deleting the period between the last two sentences and changing the first letter in "Because" to lowercase, a process that involves only a few keystrokes.

Poorer countries will be worse off than more technologically advanceo countries because they cannot control infection as well.

FIGURE 69. Correction of a fragment.

You can correct comma splices and fused sentences either by dividing the two independent units into two separate sentences or by supplying an appropriate connector between them. We could repair the comma splice in the sample paragraph as follows:

Some scientists and companies are excited about potential profits; thus they may not consider the side effects.

FIGURE 70. Correction of a comma splice.

The search function of your word processor provides additional strategies for locating and correcting fragments, comma splices, and fused sentences. We will describe these operations below.

Using the Search Function to Locate Fragments

If you have tried isolating sentences but still have trouble locating fragments, use your word processor's search function to locate "sentence beginnings" that commonly introduce fragments. We have listed some of these troublesome sentence beginnings below.

TROUBLESOME SENTENCE BEGINNINGS		
Subordinators:	**Participles:**	**Infinitives:**
Because	Being	To be
If	Having	To know
When	Seeing	To do
etc.	etc.	etc.

Often students who have persistent problems with fragments are addicted to one or several of these troublesome sentence beginnings. For instance, the use of "Being" to begin sentences often results in a fragment. Consider the following example:

Fragment: Being that genetic engineering represents a clear threat to our environment. We must make sure that this technology is used responsibly.

Correct: Since genetic engineering represents a clear threat to our environment, we must make sure that this technology is used responsibly.

Examine your sentence fragments and keep a list of their starting words. If the fragments consistently open with the same words, use your word processor's search function to locate each capitalized use of them in your paper. For example, you might set your machine to search for all instances of "Because." Remember to include the capital *B* so that the computer locates only the instances of "because" that occur at the beginnings of sentences. As you locate these sentences, make sure that each one expresses a complete thought. Edit or make a note of those that do not.

Check any sentence beginnings in the preceding list that are especially troublesome for you so that you will have a record. Add any other words that you find problematic. Use this search procedure for locating fragments only after you are aware of the particular sentence beginnings that lead you astray. Searching for all the words listed above is a waste of time. The procedure is worthwhile only when you apply it to a personalized list of words.

USING WINDOWS AND SPLIT SCREENS
If your word processor allows you to open windows or split the screen, you can store a list of problematic sentence beginnings in a separate file and display it on the screen simultaneously with the paper you are analyzing for fragments.

Using the Search Function to Locate Comma Splices

If isolating sentences from your rough draft does not help you identify comma splices, you can use the search feature of your word processor to locate these problem areas. If you know that you have a tendency to write comma splices, set your word processor to search for all the commas in the list of isolated sentences you created from your rough draft. Whenever a comma occurs in the middle of a sentence, check to see if both parts of the sentence can indeed stand alone. If they can, you have located a comma splice.

Using the Search Function to Locate Conjunctive Adverbs

Frequently students write fused sentences and comma splices when they join complete thoughts with *conjunctive adverbs*. Consider the following example:

Fused Sentence Genetic engineering represents a clear threat to our environment consequently we must make sure that this technology is used responsibly.

Comma Splice Genetic engineering represents a clear threat to our environment, consequently we must make sure that this technology is used responsibly.

Correct Genetic engineering represents a clear threat to our environment; consequently, we must make sure that this technology is used responsibly.

As the example illustrates, conjunctive adverbs that link two complete thoughts must be preceded by a semicolon and followed by a comma. Placing a comma before the conjunctive adverb creates a comma splice.

Failing to provide any punctuation before the conjunctive adverb creates a fused sentence. The most common conjunctive adverbs are listed below.

COMMON CONJUNCTIVE ADVERBS		
however	thus	furthermore
consequently	moreover	hence
therefore	also	then

If you know that you have a tendency to create fused sentences or comma splices when you use one or more of these conjunctive adverbs, you can apply your word processor's search function to locate the potentially troublesome words in your draft. For example, *however* is a conjunctive adverb responsible for many problems. You can search for *however* in your rough draft and make sure that it is not at a comma splice or fused sentence boundary. Search only for "however" with a lowercase *h* since you will not be concerned with occurrences of *however* at the beginning of sentences.

Check any words in the preceding list of conjunctive adverbs that are especially problematic for you so that you will have a record. Add any other adverbial conjunctions that you use frequently when you write. When you search for these words in rough drafts, search only for the conjunctive adverbs that have previously given you trouble.

> **USING WINDOWS AND SPLIT SCREENS**
>
> If your word processor allows you to open windows or split the screen, you can store a list of problematic conjunctive adverbs in a separate file and display it on the screen simultaneously with the paper you are analyzing for fused sentences and comma splices.

AGREEMENT: PRONOUN-ANTECEDENT AND SUBJECT-VERB

Errors in agreement can occur in many different sentence types. Even so, many of these errors involve specific word configurations that you can find with the help of your word processor. As with fragments, comma splices, and fused sentences, the word processor cannot automatically correct errors in agreement, but it can help you locate them.

Pronoun-Antecedent Agreement

Many errors in pronoun-antecedent agreement occur when the plural pronouns *they, their,* and *them* refer to singular antecedents. Consider the following example:

> Despite the federal regulations controlling genetic engineering experiments, no scientist can provide complete assurance that the gene-spliced organisms they create will remain within the lab, isolated from the environment.

In this example, the plural pronoun "they" replaces the singular antecedent "scientist," so there is a mismatch. We can correct the problem by making "scientist" plural or by substituting "he or she" for "they."

You may never use *they, their,* or *them* when the antecedent is any of the following singular pronouns:

SINGULAR PROUNOUNS			
each	everyone	everybody	everything
either	anyone	anybody	anything
neither	no one	nobody	nothing
another	one		

Incorrect: Since the federal government places few restrictions on genetic engineering researchers, each must assume responsibility for the consequences of their own experiments.

Correct: Since the federal government places few restrictions on genetic engineering researchers, each must assume responsibility for the consequences of his or her own experiments.

If you have trouble with pronoun agreement, you can catch many errors by using your word processor's search function to locate occurrences of "they," "their," and "them." As you find each occurrence, check to see that the pronoun agrees with its antecedent.

Subject–Verb Agreement

Although most college students understand the principle of subject-verb agreement, in some sentences they may overlook errors. The most troublesome situation is when the subject and verb are widely separated in the sentence and do not stand out. You can avoid this problem by beginning sentences with clear subjects and by using strong, active verbs. Writing that relies heavily on forms of the verb *be* (*am, is, are, was, were, being, been, be*) tends to lack these clear subjects and active verbs and thus is more likely to produce errors in agreement. Consider the following example:

> The assumption that the genes responsible for human intellectual makeup is subject to improvement by scientists may be sharply differed with based on experimental evidence.

This sentence will surely confuse you. If you study it carefully, however, you see that it expresses an interesting idea. The problem is that the writer does not use active verbs with clear subjects to make the idea stand out. Moreover, the sentence contains a subject–verb agreement error: the singular verb "is" does not agree with its plural subject "genes." When the subject-verb relationships are not clear, the writer is more likely to make errors in subject-verb agreement. In the following version of the sentence, we corrected this problem:

> Experimental evidence shows that scientists cannot improve human intellect by changing genetic structure.

If you consistently have problems with subject–verb agreement, work to restructure your sentences around identifiable subjects and verbs. You will achieve a stronger, clearer style with fewer errors in subject–verb agreement. Your word processor can help you in this effort if you set its search function to find forms of the verb *be* (*am, is, are, was, were, being, been, be*) in your paper. When you locate a "be" verb, use the procedure we describe above to isolate and duplicate the sentence. Rework one copy of the sentence by trying to preserve the same idea without using "be" verbs. If the new version of the sentence shows improvement over the original, delete the original and close up the paragraph. If after some effort you are unable to improve the sentence, keep the original. You need not eliminate all "be" forms but try to minimize them. If you retain "be" verbs, make sure that they agree with their subjects.

Note that the process for reducing errors in subject–verb agreement that we just described is for writers who have persistent agreement problems. If you have good control of subject–verb agreement, do not invest time in this editing procedure. If you need to use this technique, however, you will find your time well spent. Eventually, you will develop a stronger, more direct style, and you will begin to use more active verbs as you compose first drafts.

SHIFT IN PERSON

Another common problem in writing is the unwarranted use of the second-person pronouns *you* and *your* and the contraction *you're*. In conversation, we often use "you" to refer to people in general, but in writing this pronoun refers to the reader, the audience for the piece. Note the problem with "you" in the following example:

> In recent years researchers have successfully cloned animal cells. This process involves first isolating the DNA from a cell of the "parent" animal. Then, you grow from this DNA a new individual that is a genetic duplicate of the original organism.

The passage describes a process that researchers use, but the third sentence directs the reader to try the procedure. The writer could substitute either "researchers" or "scientists" for "you."

Speakers who use "you" regularly in conversation may overlook this pronoun when they proofread, since sentences that contain "you" may "sound" correct. If "you" and its related forms tend to creep into your writing, locate them, using the search function of your word processor. Since all these forms start with either a blank followed by "you" or the capitalized word "You," you can locate all potential problems involving second-person shifts with these two searches. Remember, however, that you are looking for pronoun *shifts*. You need not conduct a search if "you" is used consistently.

WORD USAGE AND VOCABULARY

Since the range of usage errors is vast, there is no simple, generalizable method to find and remedy them with a word processor. Even computer programs designed to detect usage errors do not help very much. You can minimize problems with vocabulary if you keep a running list of the words that instructors have consistently corrected in your papers. Then set your word processor to search through your drafts for these words. For instance, if you have a tendency to multiply intensifying adverbs like *really*, *very*, or *quite*, you can quickly search drafts for any occurrences of these words. You can also search for prepositions that you often misuse. One of the most troublesome prepositions is *of*. Notice the problem with "of " in the following example:

Incorrect: Recombinant DNA technology involves incorporating cells derived of one organism into the cells of another.

Correct: Recombinant DNA technology involves incorporating cells derived from one organism into the cells of another.

Use your word processor to search for any vocabulary problems that you have regularly. Maintain a textfile for storing these words.

USING WINDOWS AND SPLIT SCREENS
If your word processor allows you to open windows or split the screen, you can store a list of problematic vocabulary words in a separate file and display it on the screen simultaneously with the paper you are editing.

SPELLING

For many writers an electronic spelling checker is a special bonus in word processing. State-of-the-art word processors and even some electronic typewriters come with built-in spelling checkers. Separate spelling checkers can be purchased to complement those word processors that do not come with this feature. Most spelling checkers let you compare the spelling of words in your paper to a dictionary-based word list, usually containing 50,000 words or more. You can also use the standard search function of your word processor to check spelling. Both of these options are important, so we will discuss them separately.

Dictionary-Based Word Lists

If your rough drafts contain numerous misspellings involving many different words, check them against a dictionary-based word list. In this process, the computer will compare every word in your paper against a list of the most commonly used words in the English language. The computer will also identify words in your paper that do not appear in the list. Some of these words may need correction, but others may not. For example, the computer will flag as misspelled many proper nouns (names) and specialized words (technical terms, jargon, slang, and so on) since these less common words will not appear on the standard lists.

Many spelling checkers also allow you to create a second dictionary list containing words you use frequently or to add new words to the standard dictionary. For example, a biology student might add specialized technical terms like "monogenic" and names of prominent geneticists like "Sinsheimer" in order to check research papers on genetics. If you use a dictionary-based word list, it is essential that you tailor it to your needs. Otherwise, you will become frustrated when your machine continuously flags as incorrect words that do not contain errors.

Often, spelling checkers not only identify misspellings but also suggest options from their word lists for correct spellings. Basically, these programs search for the most likely matches between the misspelled words in your paper and the words in the program's list. With some spelling checkers the program locates the error and presents the student with several numbered options for the correct spelling. When the student types in the number of the correct spelling, the change will be made throughout the entire paper. These features are valuable to students who are either weak spellers or inaccurate typists. Dyslexic students often fall into both of these categories. We have worked with dyslexic students who cannot find words in a dictionary but who can recognize correctly spelled words when they see them. Since retyping the word will often introduce new errors into the dyslexic student's work, being able to select the number of the correct option is a tremendous advantage.

There are some difficulties with a dictionary-based spelling checker. As we mentioned above, you need to customize your spelling checker or it will flag many correct words as misspelled. Even after you customize, however, it will flag any specialized vocabulary and proper nouns you have not entered into the dictionary. In addition, some word lists have curious omissions. For example, one of our spelling checkers does not recognize "create" as a correct word. Finally, spelling checkers can be slow. Very weak spellers can spend hours checking the spelling in long papers. Still, for poor spellers, using a spelling checker is less time consuming than hunting for each misspelled word and looking it up in the dictionary.

Search-and-Replace Spelling Correction

Another way to correct your spelling is to use the search-and-replace function of your word processor to locate and correct errors you habitually make. This involves keeping a list of the words you frequently misspell. Next to each misspelling, record its correct version. For example, your list might contain the misspelling "their" coupled with its correct spelling "their." To check your errors, direct the computer to search for each misspelling on the list. As you locate each instance, use your computer's editing capacity to correct the mistake.

USING SEARCH-AND-REPLACE FILES

Some sophisticated word processors and spelling checkers allow you to establish a file that contains a list of word-for-word replacements that you want to make in other files. Using this capability you could establish a file that contains a list of the words you commonly misspell along with their correct spellings (for example, "thier" and "their"). Then you could use this file to make changes in other files that hold drafts of your papers. Once you have created a search-and-replace file, you can use it to analyze and change as many files as you may wish. Only a single command is needed to analyze and change each new file. Obviously, this process could make it easier for you to check your paper against a customized spelling list of your own.

The search-and-replace method works best for students who discover that many of their misspellings involve a small set of words. Suppose homophones, words that sound alike but have different spellings (for example, *know–no, two–to–too, whether–weather*) are your downfall. You know that you habitually confuse these homophones. Nevertheless, you pass over them as you proofread. The computer's steely-eyed search function can readily locate these potential traps. The search-and-replace method, however, is not practical for more than fifteen words. Writers with more extensive spelling problems may need to use a dictionary-based program.

Students with severe spelling problems can benefit from both the dictionary-based spelling checkers and the search-and-replace method. A combination of these two techniques will detect most of their errors.

PUNCTUATION

A word processor is not very useful for identifying punctuation errors. The machine cannot judge where punctuation marks should go within particular sentences. If you tend to overuse commas or apostrophes, you could use the word processor's search function to locate their occurrence and then check the context to see if you have used them properly. However, this electronic proofreading may be no more efficient than reading through the printed draft for punctuation marks. Unlike spelling errors, punctuation marks do stand out from the rest of the sentence, so you will notice them as you proofread visually.

CUSTOMIZING SENTENCE EDITING

It takes far longer to describe electronic proofreading techniques than it does to use them. As we mentioned earlier, however, you will waste time if you apply all of them to your writing. Select only those that speak to your particular problems as a writer. Work with a subset including techniques that enable you to edit a short paper in under an hour. As your writing improves, you may eliminate editing techniques that are no longer necessary and add new techniques that deal with more sophisticated concerns.

Finally, remember that while electronic proofreading is useful, it is not a substitute for careful editing. Electronic techniques will help you locate certain types of errors; nevertheless, they should not replace traditional proofreading methods. Ultimately it is not the machine but you who are responsible for the correctness and accuracy of your writing.

EXERCISE 8

Below is an excerpt from the first draft of a student's paper on television and society. The draft contains a number of errors in grammar, usage, and spelling. Type the draft on your word processor *exactly* as it appears below. Then, use the procedures described in Chapter 8 to locate and correct any problems with sentence boundaries, agreement, shift in person, vocabulary, and spelling.

> Perhaps the most serious problem with television is that it disrupts family life. In particular, extensive television viewing cuts down on the interaction between family members. Before television, families came together at dinner and discussed the events of the day. After dinner, family members talked or played games together. In many current American families, however, the evening hours are really dominated by the television. Many of the most popular children's programs are on between the time school ends and the dinner hour. Children often eat there dinner in front of the set and then continue watching untill bedtime. This leaves little time of interaction with parents and siblings. Since many American homes now have more than one television. Family members often spend the evening hours in entirely separate rooms watching different shows. Even when parents and children do watch together, they rarely talk during the programs or even during advertisements. Some parents conciously use the television as an electronic babysitter. So that they do not have to be bothered with their children at dinner or during the evening. Clearly, heavy television watching creates problems, less time is spent together as a family.
>
> Another problem with television is that it adversely affects both the mental development and educational progress of children. Television very much reduces a child's ability to concentrate on reading and writing. When a child who has been exposed to a lot of television reads a story without pictures. They complain and there attention wanders. Children who read more than they watch television has longer attention spans and can visualize things better in their minds. Reading gives you perception and reasoning skills. Reading broadens the mind consequently it is superior to television watching.

NINE
WORD PROCESSORS IN COMPUTERIZED CLASSROOMS AND WORD PROCESSING WORKROOMS

Today, writing laboratories, campus learning centers, computer workrooms, and even some college classrooms are equipped with word processors. This chapter will focus on the special learning opportunities these word processing centers can provide. The activities in this chapter serve as exercises to improve your work in computerized classrooms or writing labs. They may also suggest other ways to profit from the informal learning that often occurs in these situations. We have found that students who regularly use the word processing workrooms on our campuses tend to form a community of writers who help each other and learn together. The activities we describe in this chapter may prompt you to form a similar community.

Throughout this chapter we will use "computer workroom" as a cover term for any location that has a number of computer stations for word processing. The term covers a wide range of different types of facilities. The workroom may be a writing classroom wired specifically for word processing or it may be a common space that serves students working on computer programs, math, and other projects, as well as writing. Work stations may contain freestanding microcomputers or keyboards that connect to either a mainframe or a microcomputer networking system. The facility may have writing tutors, computer consultants, or both tutors and consultants, or it may be entirely unstaffed. This chapter will help writers in any of these working environments.

Underlying our approach is the belief that, whenever possible, students should collaborate as they learn to write. All writing instruction involves stages of collaboration between a student and a teacher. We encourage a further stage of collaboration among students themselves. As we pointed out earlier, students in computer workrooms tend to aid one another. In business, industry, and various professions writing projects routinely involve the combined efforts of several individuals. For years practitioners and theorists have recognized the value of collaborative writing as an instructional technique. In fact, Kenneth Bruffee has developed an approach to writing instruction based largely on collaborative methods.* In this chapter we will explain how computerized classrooms and word processing workrooms make it possible for writers to pool resources at all stages of the writing process.

Although many writing teachers endorse collaborative learning, we must caution you that this approach is not universally accepted; some professors, particularly those in fields other than English composition, may insist that you work entirely alone. Other instructors may require you to acknowledge all the assistance you receive on papers, including help from college-supported writing centers. And some instructors may judge any form of collaboration as academically dishonest. *Make sure you know how your instructor views collaborative writing before you use the techniques in this chapter to work on papers for a particular course.* Also, be aware that some forms of collaboration border on plagiarism and are inappropriate in academic writing. For example, you should never borrow phrases or ideas from someone else without giving that person proper credit. Above all, collaboration must never be an excuse for getting someone else to do your work for you. Collaboration should provide you with a critical and helpful audience, but control over the writing process must remain firmly in your own hands.

HARDWARE AND SOFTWARE COMPATIBILITY

In many of the collaborative writing activities that we describe in this chapter a student produces a draft of a paper at one word processing work station, and then an instructor or peer reviewer comments on the draft at a different station. Switching from one work station or one word processing program to another can cause problems of compatibility. If you and someone else intend to work together, both your hardware (microcomputer or computer terminal) and your software

* Kenneth Bruffee, "Collaborative Learning: Some Practical Methods," *College English* 34 (1973): 634–43.

(word processing program) must be compatible. Your hardware will be compatible if you both use terminals that are connected to a single large computer or if you use *identical* microcomputers. Your software will be compatible if you both use *exactly the same* version of a word processing program. When both hardware and software are compatible, you should have no trouble exchanging textfiles electronically through a network or by swapping floppy disks. Be sure you make backup copies of disks before you exchange. If you use different types of computers, different word processing software packages, or different versions of the same software package, you will very likely run into problems when you attempt to exchange files. Within a particular manufacturer's product line all models may not run the same software. Even when computers are marketed as "clones" (exact copies of popular name-brand computers), there are some differences that may affect word processing functions. In short, you and your collaborator should try to use only one make and model of computer and only one version of a particular word processing program.

If you are knowledgeable about computers, you may be able to overcome these problems of capability. Translation programs exist that allow you to pass data from one type of computer to another, and some word processors are set up to handle textfiles created by other programs. Nevertheless, these transfer processes can be complex and unwieldy. Before you begin a writing project that involves transfers of this sort, make sure that you understand fully what will be involved in exchanging textfiles. Test out the exchange procedure and see that it works. *Back up all disks before they are translated or exchanged.*

PREWRITING

Electronic Conversations*

When you are exploring the possibilities of a topic, you can discover ideas by having an "electronic conversation" with a fellow student. One of the best ways to generate ideas is through a dialogue that involves taking

* We are indebted to our colleague Barbara Adams at Ithaca College who introduced us to the idea of an electronic conversation. Professor Adams uses the technique to help students become familiar with the keyboard.

positions, receiving criticism and support, listening to different views, and responding to the ideas of others. An electronic conversation proceeds exactly like a spoken conversation, except that statements are typed on the word processor rather than spoken.

To conduct an electronic conversation, you and your partner should follows these steps:

CONDUCTING AN ELECTRONIC CONVERSATION

1. Sit at adjacent computer work stations.
2. Insert a personal disk into the computer (if necessary), start up a word processing program, and begin a new textfile.
3. Exchange keyboards so that what you type will appear on your partner's screen and what he or she types will appear on your screen. (Note that you will have to modify this procedure if your computer keyboard is attached permanently to other parts of the work station).
4. Use the word processors to interchange remarks on the assigned topic, just as you would in a regular conversation, but *do not speak.* You need not worry about correctness, but your writing should make sense. An electronic conversation helps stimulate your thinking just as a good discussion does, but it also provides you with a record of your thoughts.
5. Continue the activity until the "conversation" arrives at a natural endpoint.
6. Switch places once more so that you can see on the screen the textfile you typed.
7. Save this file. You can now use this material as a source of ideas just as you would freewriting notes (see Chapter 2).

Interactive freewriting not only results in a creative interchange of ideas, it also reaps the benefits of "invisible writing." As we explained in Chapter 2, not being able to see what you are typing can free you from worrying about detail and thus help you focus more directly on generating ideas.

NETWORKING SYSTEMS

If you have a networking system that allows you to send messages from one terminal to another, you could develop a variation of interactive freewriting that involves an electronic conversation among three or more individuals. The possibilities here will depend on the precise capacities of your system.

Commenting on Prewriting Notes

In Chapter 2 we mentioned the desirability of having instructors or peers comment on your prewriting notes. Instructors often collect prewriting journals so that they can identify ideas that could be developed into full papers, point out ideas that need further development, suggest alternative approaches, and register other comments. Sometimes course journals and prewriting notes are also reviewed by peers. Students usually submit these notes and journals in handwritten form. But they can just as easily submit floppy disks containing their prewriting textfiles or pass textfiles to reviewers through a networking system. This method is less cumbersome and, if students back up their files, safer than exchanging handwritten notes. In addition, it is easier to comment on prewriting that has been done on a word processor. Handwritten notes, often done rapidly, may be illegible, whereas material on the word processor screen is always easy to read. In addition, a reviewer may have little room in the margin for comments on handwritten notes, but he or she can create new lines in the middle of a textfile and add as many comments as desired.

One way to insert a comment in prewriting notes is to move the cursor to the point where the comment is relevant, add extra lines, and then type the comment, indented and in capital letters, so that it stands out clearly. Note how this is done in Betsy Fowlson's notes.

```
Our house is on a quiet country road. Other houses are
        WHAT'S THE NAME OF THE ROAD?
close by, but they are not visible to us because there are many trees
surrounding them. A unique feature of the neighborhood
        WHAT TYPES OF TREES HIDE THE HOUSES?
is a babbling brook that runs adjacent to our property. This brook is
popular in the summer, as it s a cooling-off spot for the children who live
```

up and down the road. The neighborhood includes many families with school-aged children. In addition, within a short distance from our house is a woman called Miss King who lives alone and is now eighty. Miss King is a retired schoolteacher who lives alone and does not have any relatives. We in the neighborhood became her family. Her yard is the best

I LIKE THIS IDEA. COULD YOU TELL US MORE ABOUT HOW YOU AND YOUR NEIGHBORS BECAME MISS KING'S ADOPTED FAMILY? WHAT DOES THIS INVOLVE? WHAT OTHER CONTACT DO YOU HAVE WITH HER? ARE THERE OTHER TIMES WHEN THE CHILDREN VISIT HER?

FIGURE 71. Example of comments in prewriting notes.

sledding hill around, so she always has company when the children get home from school. Miss King, or Elizabeth, as the adults call her, is interesting and well-traveled. The road we live on, King Road, is named after Elizabeth's family, who once

YES, ELIZABETH SOUNDS LIKE A VERY INTERESTING FOCUS. TELL US MORE ABOUT HER. YOU MIGHT TELL US HOW KING ROAD HAS EVOLVED OVER THE YEARS.

owned all the land in the area.

FIGURE 71. (continued)

In the example above, we stressed analyzing the content of prewriting material. For personal essays and other "creative" writing assignments, however, analyzing "voice" may also be important at the prewriting stage.* We use "voice" to refer to the overall impression, the "feel" the reader gets from the writing. Voice is strong when the writing appears authentic and fresh, when it shows life and rhythm. Compare the following two passages, the first lifeless, the second with voice.

* In this book we use the term *voice* to refer to the resonance of writing. See Peter Elbow, *Writing with Power* (New York: Oxford University Press, 1981). "Voice" also has a grammatical meaning that you will find in a style manual.

In the suburban town in New Jersey where I live the ranch houses are about 200 feet apart. Behind many of the houses are manicured lawns, gardens, patios, and pools. From the front the houses are strikingly similar, yet the families who live in my neighborhood are not at all alike. On my block alone there are six familes that are very different. To the left of my house are the Santinis, a family of three generations: grandparents, parents, and three teenagers. To my right are the Bigsbys, two middle-aged sisters who are accountants. The three ranches across the street house the Penners, the O'Rourkes, and the Gebhards.

FIGURE 72. Example of lifeless prose.

Up until the time I was about seven or eight, we had a fourteen-foot above-ground pool in our backyard. Not much, granted, but to a bunch of hot, sweaty kids, it was an oasis. Our house was "that house on the block" in the Kool-Aid commercial. Somehow, by the end of each day, my mother wound up with three times as many kids as she started with: three Assengs, two O'Loughlins, two Cippolas, three Mittlemans, five Washburns, and her own McGuires to boot. Mom liked everybody except Billy Washburn whom she called a "snot-nosed, obnoxious, big-mouthed bully." That summed up Billy very nicely and many of us shared Mom's view.

FIGURE 73. Example of prose with voice (by Sheila McGuire).

As you read through prewriting notes, you can comment on voice just as we commented on content above. Notice how the reviewer makes helpful comments on Besty Fowlson's notes.

Bobby had his share of difficulties growing up, difficulties I shared with my twin brother. Bobby struggled through elementary school. The more he failed, the more adamant he became against school work. But eventually he realized that he must learn how to read or his life would continue to be a hardship. I was proud the day he brought our younger sister's book to my room and said simply, "Betsy, help me read this." I cooperated just as simply, keeping all the exclamations about how "it was about time" and "he had finally come to his senses" to myself. Bobby needed encouragement, not admonishment. We spent many hours in the attic, hiding from the other nine members of our chaotic family, diligently working on Bobby's reading skills.

BETSY, I LIKE THIS. I CAN PICTURE THE SCENE AND I HAVE A GOOD SENSE OF YOUR FEELINGS. IN THIS PARAGRAPH, YOUR VOICE IS COMING ACROSS LOUD AND CLEAR.

To this day he does not want any pat on the back for his determination and perseverance, but he knows he accomplished a great deal that year.

FIGURE 74. Example of comments on voice.

We all applaud the formally educated person, the person with a bachelor's, master's, or doctorate. Everyone is proud of his or her accomplishments. On the other hand, the person who attains knowledge and success on his or her own is often overlooked. Many exceptionally wise and perceptive adults learn through real-life experiences and not in a classroom.

BETSY, IN THIS PARAGRAPH, I AM LOSING VOICE. TRY TO BREATHE MORE OF YOURSELF INTO THESE WORDS. PERSONALIZE YOUR COMMENTS ABOUT FORMALLY EDUCATED VS. SELF-EDUCATED PEOPLE. TALK ABOUT BOBBY.

FIGURE 74. (continued)

Note that comments on prewriting should be limited to content, voice, completeness, logic, organization, and other global issues and should not cover matters of correctness. Focus on idea development, not spelling, grammar, or usage. If several reviewers comment on a single paper, each reviewer should add his or her initials after the comments so that the writer can distinguish between the reviews. The reviewer should also date comments if the entries in a writer's journal or other prewriting notes are themselves dated.

DRAFTING

A major advantage of drafting papers in a word processing workroom is that you are in the company of other writers who can comment on your work as you compose. The advice you get *as* you draft can be just as valuable as feedback you receive on a completed paper. As you draft, your questions may be as simple as asking someone whether a particular sentence makes sense, or they may involve more complex issues such as whether or not the thesis is consistent with the rest of the paper. As we pointed out in Chapter 4, the process of drafting may lead you to develop alternative arguments or even to change your approach entirely. Drafting involves much more than converting notes into words; it is a creative activity that may give rise to new ideas about the topic and also to new questions about content, organization, or correctness. If your computer workroom is part of a writing lab or learning center, writing tutors may be available to advise you as you work. Informal writers' groups, classmates, and friends are other possible sources of help.

Writing instructors often require students to work on their rough drafts in workshops where they can get help from instructors and peers. Word processing workrooms are ideal locations for such classes. The clear, legible computer display makes it easy for instructors or peers to read quickly over sections of your draft, and the editing capabilities of the word processor help you to make changes based on their feedback.

REVISING

The goals of collaborative revision are to improve papers and, more importantly, to produce better writers. Collaborative revision does not mean that a strong writer cleans up the work of a weaker writer. It means instead that a reviewer helps a writer locate problems that the writer can then work to solve. The reviewer in turn comes to see why those problems distort communication. Both the writer and the reviewer learn from this process.

At the revising stage collaboration may focus on a single aspect of writing or on several aspects. For instance, a reviewer might scan a rough draft, looking only at paragraph transition. In other cases a reviewer might scroll through a draft and then provide feedback on idea development, organization, and style. Notice the various approaches in the following example. Here are excerpts from an assignment that requires the student to conduct a personal interview. Carrie Miller has recorded quotations from her subject, Dr. Arnold and she has woven them into her rough draft.

Dr. Arnold walked toward his desk, sat down, and said, "My own parents both worked out, and we had a housekeeper." He was

> CARRIE, YOU NEED TO DEVELOP THESE IDEAS ABOUT THE PARENTS AND THE HOUSEKEEPER AND CONNECT THEM TO THE REST OF THE PARAGRAPH.

very close to one of his sisters. "I remember sitting on Alison's bed sorting movie star pictures." **** YOU NEED A CONNECTING IDEA HERE **** "You're too young to remember the radio shows 'Stars Over Hollywood' and 'Grand Central Station.'"

> YOU JUMP FROM THE RADIO SHOWS TO DR. ARNOLD'S JOB. ADD A CONNECTING IDEA OR TRANSITION.

"I was a milkman, at one time, somewhere between pasteurized and homogenized. You drove a stand-up milk truck then." Dr. Arnold smiled as he is remembering the job and the early morning hours of quiet delivery and [being done by noon]. **** THIS DOESN'T SOUND RIGHT **** His voice seemed to be saying, "Oh yes, those were the days."

Figure 75. A collaborative revision.

A bit of excitement came into his voice and his eyebrows rose as if to imply that what he was about to tell me was incredible but true. "When I was in the army, it was during the

> CARRIE, THE FIRST SENTENCE IN THIS PARAGRAPH LETS ME HEAR AND SEE DR. ARNOLD. COULD YOU WRITE MORE SENTENCES LIKE THIS ONE? THAT WAY YOUR PAPER WOULD SOUND MORE LIKE A PORTRAIT OF DR. ARNOLD AND LESS LIKE AN INTERVIEW.

[Cuban Missile Crisis]. **** WILL YOUR AUDIENCE NEED A DATE TO PLACE THIS EVENT? **** There I was at the southern tip of Florida; I could picture myself just like Teddy Roosevelt charging up San Juan Hill; you know the picture in the school books?" He tipped his desk chair back as he was thinking deeply. "I can hardly believe it myself," he said as his voice trailed off. **** WHERE? ****

Figure 75. (continued)

The reviewer places brackets around problematic phrases or sentences, indents and capitalizes long comments, and highlights short comments with asterisks and capitalization. The reviewer does not change the draft, but rather provides advice and indicates where problems may lie. It is up to the writer to decide what specific changes need to be made.

A writer who wants feedback on a rough draft should follow the procedure given below.

OBTAINING FEEDBACK ON A ROUGH DRAFT

1. The writer makes a backup copy of a draft textfile and then passes the textfile to the reviewer either on a floppy disk or through an electronic networking system.
2. The reviewer comments electronically on the draft. The reviewer then saves the annotated file *under a new textfile name.* The textfile containing the writer's original draft must be left intact.
3. When the reviewer finishes the commentary, he or she returns the original textfile to the writer along with the annotated file.
4. The writer either prints both files and compares them or simultaneously views both files on the computer screen using a split screen or similar word processor features.
5. The writer considers the reviewer's advice and makes any changes that are appropriate in the paper draft. Then the writer removes the capitalized comments, brackets, and asterisks that the reviewer inserted.

Of course, this procedure can be modified to allow for comments from several reviewers on a single draft.

Note that many of the revising activities we described in Chapters 5 through 7 can be adapted for collaborative revision. For instance, if you are unsure that you have sustained your focus, you might, as we suggest on page 81, produce a version of the paper that includes a nutshell of the main idea, the introduction, and the conclusion. Then, ask one or more reviewers to judge whether or not the focus is consistent throughout this version. Revising activities like this one work well for class workshops. Instructors can individualize the workshops by tailoring them to their students' writing weaknesses. The students themselves can recommend the revising strategies that will be beneficial.

Collaborative revision also lends itself to in-class exercises. For example, the instructor can create a textfile that contains a sample paper and give it to students, either by having them copy the file to their own floppy disks or by transfering the file through a networking system. Working individually or in small groups, students can review the sample paper according to the instructor's directions. For example, they might determine the writer's organizational plan, look for cohesive devices, analyze sentence length, or search for ineffective expressions. Finally, the entire class can discuss the results of this analysis.

EDITING

Within a computerized classroom, some instructors may use peer editing exercises similar to the peer revising exercises we described above. Usually, peer editing exercises are designed to help teach or reinforce principles of correctness. Note that the purpose of these exercises is to help students become more independent rather than to make them rely on others for corrections. When one student merely proofreads another student's work, no learning takes place, and the instructor may legitimately question the honesty of both students. Thus, it is best to keep peer editing within a supervised classroom or writing lab. If you feel that you have a good reason to receive proofreading help, discuss the situation with your instructor.

JOINT WRITING PROJECTS

As we mentioned earlier, in business, industry, and the professions writers often collaborate. To prepare students for collaborative writing tasks, some college professors assign writing projects to teams of students rather than to individuals. Group writing assignments are popular in the social sciences and in business courses since teamwork is important in those fields.

Word processors are very useful for group writing projects. If group members do their prewiting and drafting on compatible word processors, they can easily comment on each other's work. In cases where each writer works on a separate part of the project, word processors make it easy to combine all the parts. Some specific collaborative activities that you might try when you are working on joint writing projects are listed below.

TECHNIQUES FOR JOINT WRITING PROJECTS

1. Divide the topic into manageable subunits and have group members compose the first draft of their assigned

subsections. Then transfer all the textfiles to a single disk. (There should be a program on your operating system disk that will help you transfer textfiles from disk to disk.) Next, combine all the subsections into a single textfile and have each person review the text and add comments. Discuss any differences of opinion and work together to produce a complete draft of the paper.

2. For shorter assignments have each group member write a complete version of the paper. Print out and compare the versions, and decide which parts of each version you want to retain. Then transfer all the textfiles to a single disk, and combine the usable parts to form a single draft of the paper. Revise this file carefully so that the draft is unified, coherent, and cohesive.

ESSAY EXAMINATIONS

Increasingly, college professors are administering examinations in word processing workrooms. The advantage for the professor is that essay exams done on a word processor are legible and easy to grade. The advantage for students is that they can use the word processor's revising capabilities to write better-organized and more complete papers.

Students with physical handicaps or learning disabilities may write exams on word processors as part of alternative testing arrangements. These students use word processing technology to help compensate for handicaps that interfere with their performance on tests. For instance, a dyslexic student with spelling irregularities makes his or her paper easier to read and therefore earns a higher grade for content and ideas when he or she eliminates distracting misspellings with a spelling checker. In addition, some physically handicapped students find it easier to type than to write out their examinations. Visually impaired students may use special word processing software that displays a text with large-print letters that are easy to read. All these word processing features help minimize the extent to which students' handicaps interfere with their performance on essay exams.

EXERCISE 9

Collaborative Invention

1. Pair up with another student and sit at adjacent terminals in your word processing workroom
2. Agree upon a topic on which you will both write. Then carry on an electronic

conversation on this topic, according to the procedure we describe on page 150. Produce about 500 words apiece.

3. After the electronic conversation is finished, comment on each other's free-writing as we describe on pages 151–154. In particular, try to identify promising ideas for further development.
4. Revise your writing based on the comments you received. Expand ideas the reviewer liked and delete ideas the reviewer felt were weak.
5. Print out your revised material. Read your printout and then exchange with your partner and read his or her work. Discuss which ideas are the strongest in both revisions and which ideas are weakest. Look for patterns that could be used to combine your ideas.
6. Merge your two idea files and revise the combined file to form a clustered idea list (see page 24) that could form the basis for a paper draft.

APPENDIX—SOFTWARE AND HARDWARE

This appendix describes the hardware and software components of word processing systems. We discuss both standard word processors and add-ons that can expand the functions of your computer and software. Our goal is to show how you can choose specific equipment and programs to customize your word processing system to your own needs. In addition, we suggest criteria for making purchasing decisions. Whenever we mention brand names of hardware and software, we do not mean to endorse specific products. Rather, our purpose is to point out illustrative examples. We have provided addresses of manufactures to whom you can write for more detailed information.

COMPUTERS

Numerous articles in both the popular press and specialized journals advise consumers on how to shop for computers. Keep in mind that these articles often focus on advanced hardware features that have little impact on word processing capabilities. A state-of-the-art computer may make your word processing more efficient and will certainly provide more opportunities for you beyond word processing. Still, a fairly limited and relatively inexpensive computer that is nonetheless adequate for word processing may be your best bet in the long run. For instance, the entire manuscript for this book was outlined, drafted, and revised on an inexpensive 64K machine. Each individual must consider the tradeoff between speed, power and versatility, on the one hand, and price, on the other.

For those interested primarily in word processing, perhaps the best purchasing strategy is to look for software first and then buy the machine that runs the software you want to use. As a rule, modern computer hardware is reliable, but software varies greatly in quality and function. A top-notch computer will do you little good if it cannot run the programs you find most useful. Always consider software cost before you buy hardware. In some cases, the cost of the software may exceed the cost of the computer itself. Consumers are drawn to the hardware-software packages available from most dealers, but remember that unless you are comfortable using the word processing program that comes with your hardware, the package deal provides no real advantage. Make sure you try out the word processing program that the dealer offers you and compare it to other programs.

In order to reduce hardware costs, buyers often choose "clones," relatively inexpensive copies of popular computer brands. Although many of the newer clones are faithful copies of the original machines, it is important to check that the clone will run the specific software you are interested in using. Subtle differences in construction may mean that the clone will not perform all word processing functions exactly as does the machine for which the software was originally designed. In most instances, however, the clone will run the software successfully and operate just as effectively as the brand-name computer.

There are advantages to buying a computer that is compatible with the machines in the computer workroom on your campus. For example, when your own equipment breaks down in the middle of a writing project, you can take your diskettes to a college computer and continue working. Some students compose on their own computers and then use the campus hardware to print out a letter-quality final draft. In addition, colleges often have special purchasing arrangements with their hardware suppliers to let faculty members and students buy computers at special discounts.

Of course, many students and faculty members never purchase their own computers but rather use the computing facilities on their campuses for word processing. In addition to saving the purchase price of a computer, there are at least two other advantages to using campus computer workrooms. If you are using a college computer, you will have access to the college's library of writing software, materials that might cost you thousands of dollars to purchase on your own. If you use a college mainframe computer for word processing, you may be able to sample more complex word processing software that will run only on large computers.

WORD PROCESSING PROGRAMS

As we mentioned above, finding the word processing program that suits you may be more important than finding the best computer. Word processing software varies dramatically in terms of the function and the ease of operation. Our experience shows that state-of-the-art word processors with a great variety of features are not necessarily the best for all users. Features that greatly assist the skilled user may confuse the novice, and even skilled users often ignore complex word processing operations. On the other hand, some popular word processors are so limited that they cannot handle many of the operations we describe in this book. A word processor should perform all the operations we discussed in Chapter 1. When you try out a new word processor, run through the activities in Exercise 1 (page 15). This exercise reviews the essential word processing functions. A good word processor should allow you to accomplish all the operations described in this exercise without going through an awkward series of commands.

Below is a list of additional factors you should consider before you buy a word processor:

- Ease of operation: Is it easy to perform the basic editing operations? Can you save and print files without difficulty?
- Hardware requirements: What computer brands and models will run the program? How much core memory is needed to run the program? Is a special monitor or option card (circuit board) needed to take full advantage of the program's features?
- Software requirements: What operating system (DOS, MS-DOS, and so on) is needed to support the program? Will you need to purchase this operating system separately, and if so what will it cost? (Typically, computers come with an operating system as part of the purchase price. Operating systems can be quite expensive when purchased separately.)
- Ease of learning: based on skimming the manual, does it seem that you will be able to learn the system easily and quickly?
- Spelling checker: Does the word processing program have a built-in spelling checker? If not, will you be able to obtain a spelling checker that works in conjunction with the word processor?
- Special requirements: Do you need special word processing features, such as the ability to include graphics within your documents? (Note that the need for graphics may also affect hardware and printer requirements).

Recently, several publishers have come out with simplified word processors that include just the features most useful to college students. They are designed so that students can quickly learn to prepare essays and research papers without being confused by complex word processing operations they will not need. In general, these programs cost less than a typical college textbook. In addition to a simplified word processor, these programs usually include special features that will help the college writer. For instance, the PRENTICE-HALL COLLEGE WRITER allows the writer on-line access to advice about grammar, style, and mechanics. The program also includes a "notes" feature that provides a workspace for outlining and other prewriting activities and a "comments" feature that allows the instructor or other students to append "invisible" comments to specific parts of the paper draft. The writer can, on a split screen, simultaneously view the draft and either the notes or the comments. Two of these college word processing programs are listed below:

Prentice-Hall College Writer (for IBM PC)
Prentice-Hall, Inc.
College Book Division, Englewood Cliffs, NJ 07632

Wordperfect: The McGraw-Hill College Version (for IBM-PC)
Marketing Manager for Computing,
27th Floor
1221 Avenue of the Americas
New York, NY 10020

PRINTERS

It is common for dealers to offer both a computer and a printer in a single package. The dealer can make sure that the printer is compatible with the computer, and costs can be lower. While some printers can work with many different computers, others are designed to work with only a few models. The interaction between the printer and your word processing software is also crucial. Make sure that you see your computer, software, and printer all working together before you make your purchase. Ask your dealer if your software needs to be "configured" or altered before it will work with your printer. Get the dealer to help you with the configuration if it seems complex. Make sure that the dealer tells you how to connect the computer to the printer, and ask for the dealer's help if the process seems difficult.

It is advisable to get a good printer for college-level work. Many professors will not accept computer printouts of poor quality. If you want a dot-matrix printer, get one with a "letter quality" option and check a sample of it before you buy. Another reason to invest in a good printer is that, of all the elements of your word processing system, the printer is most likely to malfunction. While the electronics of modern computers are realtively trouble free, the mechanical parts of a printer are subject to wear and failure. Find out if your dealer can guarantee service on the printer you buy.

Some electronic typewriters can double as computer printers. These typewriters may hook directly to a computer or may require a special interface. The machine can still be used as a conventional typewriter when you are not printing from the computer. If you need a new typewriter as well as a printer, you should definitely consider this option. However, typewriters are often very slow when they function as printers.

As we mentioned earlier, you can get by without a printer if your computer is compatible with other machines on campus. In this case, you merely compose and revise on your own computer screen and take your disk to your campus computer center when you need hard copy. Some students own an inexpensive printer that they use for rough drafts and rely on the college printer for final drafts.

INVENTION PROGRAMS

Invention programs provide exercises, heuristics, directed questions, and other activities that help stimulate writers' thinking as they explore a topic. They can help students to generate new ideas and then to structure these ideas around a central purpose. Many of these programs are computerized versions of standard invention techniques that are commonly suggested in composition textbooks. However, the computer programs are usually interactive and thus can individualize invention techniques in response to the user's input. Below are examples of invention programs:

Creative Problem Solving (IBM and Apple)
Raymond Rodrigues
Office of the Vice-President
Colorado State University
Fort Collins, CO 80523

Organize (IBM and Apple)
Wadsworth Publishing Company
10 Davis Drive
Delmont, CA 94002

IDEA PROCESSORS

Idea processors provide the means to manipulate prewriting notes or outlines with ease. The more sophisticated programs allow the user to move rapidly back and forth among blocks of information. This can facilitate seeing patterns in ideas and reorganizing material according to these patterns. Since the programs help writers to regroup ideas quickly, they provide the flexibility to try out a variety of organizational patterns. Examples of idea processors are given below:

More (Macintosh)
Living Videotext
117 Easy Street
Mountain View, CA 94043

PC-Outline (IBM)
SoftWorks Development
750 Stierlin Road, #142
Mountain View, CA 94043

TEXT ANALYSIS PROGRAMS

These programs analyze drafts of papers according to set criteria and then advise writers on revising and editing. Often they flag potential errors in the text of the paper and also provide summary analyses of general stylistic characteristics. The program may guide the user through a standard analysis process, or it may allow the user to select options from a list of analytic functions. Typically, the program searches for grammar and usage problems by looking for word patterns that are often associated with errors. For example, the program might highlight occurrences of "their is" as probable errors. It may analyze a particular style by compiling statistics, such as average sentence length, overall readibility level, distribution of sentence type, and frequency of passive-voice constructions. Some programs compare the style of a student's paper with that of a model passage.

Before you purchase a text analysis program, make sure that it is compatible with your hardware and software. Grammar and style checkers are often idiosyncratic. Surprisingly, one of the best-known text analysis programs will not interact with any of the popular word processing programs.

It is important to recognize the limits of text analysis programs. As we point out in Chapters 7 and 8, no computer program will correct or even locate all your stylistic weaknesses and grammar errors. These programs merely search for those difficulties that can be readily reduced to simple rules. This covers only a fraction of the important stylistic and grammar issues. Although the computer programs can provide useful advice, they by no means solve all problems with correctness or style.

Examples of text analysis programs include:

Homer (for Apple)
Charles Scribner's Sons
115 Fifth Avenue
New York, NY 10003

Critique (for IBM mainframes)
Stephen Richardson
IBM Watson Research Center
Yorktown Heights, NY 10598

SPELLING CHECKERS

If you are considering a spelling checker, try it out very thoroughly. Some of these programs are extremely awkward to use. For example, certain spelling checkers will not save any corrections until you work through all flagged words, and thus you cannot interrupt the work session until you have reviewed all potential misspellings. In addition, you can lose entire documents in the process of checking spelling. With one word processor–spelling checker combination we used in class, many more students lost files while using the spelling checker than while typing or revising. Also note the speed of spelling checkers you are considering, as they vary tremendously.

Some spelling checkers are paired with an on-line thesaurus that can provide synonyms for specific words in the text of a paper. Thesauruses can also be purchased separately.

Two spelling checkers are listed below:

Sensible Speller (Apple)
210 South Woodward
Suite 22a
Birmingham, MI 48011

Spelling Coach (Macintosh)
Deneba Software
7855 N.W. Twelfth Street
Suite 202
Miami, FL 33126

INTEGRATED WRITING PROCESS PROGRAMS

Certain programs are designed to assist writers at the various stages of the writing process. In addition to typical word processing functions, they provide features like invention assistance and text analysis. Examples of integrated writing processing programs include the following:

HBJ Writer (IBM and Apple)
Harcourt Brace Jovanovich
College Division
1250 Sixth Avenue
San Diego, CA 92101

Macproof (Macintosh)
Automated Language Processing Systems
295 Chipeta Way
Salt Lake City, UT 84108

SOFTWARE AND HARDWARE FOR DISABLED STUDENTS

For writers who are physically handicapped or have learning disabilities, computer technology can make the entire writing process much easier. Word processing systems for the disabled may be composed of a judicious selection of commonly available hardware and software and may also include specially designed components. For example, a system for a visually impaired student might provide a conventional word processor and spelling checker, a specially designed speech synthesis device that pronounces the words on the screen, and a special printer that produces documents in braille. Designing such a system may require the services of one or more specialists with knowledge of computer engineering, the nature of handicapping conditions, and the product lines available. The organizations listed below can direct disabled individuals to the agencies and companies that will provide expert advice and technical assistance:

American Foundation for the Blind, Inc.
15 West Sixteenth Street
New York, NY 10011

Association for Children and Adults with Learning Disabilities
4156 Library Road
Pittsburgh, PA 15234

The Orton Dyslexia Society
24 York Road
Baltimore, MD 21204

MEMORY TYPEWRITERS

Memory typewriters offer many features of a word processor at a relatively low cost. Some memory typewriters include screens that can display up to ten lines of text, revising and editing capabilities, diskette storage systems, and spelling checkers. They provide the additional advantage of serving as a conventional typewriter. College students who live in cramped dorm rooms or apartments may find memory typewriters convenient because they take up little room and can be stored under a bed or desk. The disadvantages of memory typewriters are that they are inflexible and cannot be readily expanded or updated. Examples of memory typewriters are listed below.

Smith Corona Personal Word Processor
839 Route 13 South
Box 2020
Cortland, NY 13045

Brother Word Processor
Typewriter Division
Box 159
Piscataway, NJ 08854

INSTRUCTIONAL SOFTWARE

Writing centers and learning laboratories often provide software for computer-assisted, self-paced instruction that covers a range of writing skills. Typically, these programs are used to supplement work within a particular course or to remedy specific deficits. Below are listed two instructional software packages:

English Microlab
Houghton Mifflin, Inc.
College Division
1 Beacon Street
Boston, MA 02107

Grammarlab
Little, Brown & Co.
34 Beacon Street
Boston, MA 02106

MAGAZINES AND JOURNALS THAT DISCUSS WORD PROCESSING HARDWARE AND SOFTWARE

Various magazines and professional journals review and advertise word processing hardware and software. Many of these publications are directed at a mass market and are available at newsstands. Others, including the following two journals, are intended for academic computer users.

Academic Computing
P.O. Box 804
McKinney, TX 75069

The Computer-Assisted Composition Journal
Methodist College
Fayetteville, NC 28301-1499

INDEX